Metafictional Characters in Modern Drama

Metafictional Characters in Modern Drama

June Schlueter

Columbia University Press : New York : 1979

The Andrew W. Mellon Foundation, through a special grant, has assisted the Press in publishing this volume.

Library of Congress Cataloging in Publication Data

Schlueter, June.
    Metafictional characters in modern drama.

    Bibliography: p.
    Includes index.
    1. Drama—20th century—History and criticism.
2. Characters and characteristics in literature.
I. Title.
PN1861.S3   809.2'9'27   79-4207
ISBN 0-231-04752-5

Columbia University Press
New York   Guildford, Surrey

For my parents,
Erna and Al Mayer,
with love

◈Contents

ᏚᏎ Acknowledgments

I THANK MY husband Paul, my friend Elaine Hallett, and my professors, Martin Meisel and Robert Egan, for this book.

My interest in self-conscious drama was first stimulated by Robert Egan in a graduate seminar at Columbia University. Under the direction of Professors Meisel and Egan, I developed many of the ideas discussed in that course into a doctoral dissertation, and later revised the manuscript into its present form.

My debt to Elaine Hallett began nearly ten years ago and will continue far beyond the publication of this book, for it was she who, through countless conversations and exchanges of correspondence, has been responsible for my developing a critical perspective toward literature. More importantly, Elaine has nurtured in me a vision of life which I shall always value, and though as a confirmed medievalist she would hardly be flattered by a "thank you" for a book on modern drama, I must nonetheless acknowledge her special and immeasurable help.

My debt to my husband Paul, which is an ongoing one, has been accruing for several years, during which time his extensive knowledge of and great love for literature have been a constant source of stimulation. Where Elaine taught me what not to look for in contemporary literature, Paul taught me what to see, and I am convinced that this book could not have been written were it not for him. He has been a patient listener and reader, a severe though fair critic and editor, and, above all, an inspiration as teacher, scholar, and friend.

I am also grateful to Marilyn Kastenhuber for offering her

x　　　**Acknowledgments**

time to type the final draft of this manuscript, and to Lafayette College for providing the funds for this expense. The Handke chapter was published in slightly different form in *Comparative Drama*, 11 (Summer 1977), and I thank the journal for permission to reprint it.

Metafictional Characters in Modern Drama

Then tell me where is Faust?
Where does he begin? Where does he end?
Is he a fiction? . . .
He is real and false at the same time.

Michel de Ghelderode,
The Death of Doctor Faust

ℐℛⅠntroduction

Self-Conscious Art

IN HIS RESPONSE to the 1971–72 Lincoln Center production of Peter Handke's *The Ride Across Lake Constance*, theater critic John Simon, with obvious displeasure, asks: "When is a play not a play but a fraud? When, in fact, is any so-called work of art not a work of art but a piece of trickery, a hoax, a nonsensical game, a fraud?"[1] The question is a valid one (though I do not think it applicable to Handke) and one which is particularly worth asking with respect to much art of the modern age. In any artistic medium—Escher and Warhol in painting, Barthelme and Robbe-Grillet in fiction—we can find the artist skillfully operating on multiple planes, teasing the mind by alternately concealing and revealing images, exposing his art even as he is creating it.

Are these artists charlatans, successful only in an ostentatious display of craft which disguises their inability as artists? Does an artist's preoccupation with his own art to the point where form becomes content constitute fraud? And if we ask these questions of *some* artists, should we not also ask them of Faulkner, Joyce, and Beckett, well-established practitioners responsible for invaluable innovations in literary form? Like Simon, I have difficulty accepting Claes Oldenburg's digging of a hole in Central Park—or, for that matter, Christo Javacheff's erecting of a twenty-four-mile nylon fence in California—as art in any sense of the word, but I am less ready than Simon to declare sheer trickery art which is concerned with itself.

1

One of the most valuable studies of self-conscious art to appear thus far is Robert Alter's *Partial Magic: The Novel as a Self-Conscious Genre*. While that study does not claim completeness, it nonetheless offers a necessary balance to F. R. Leavis' well-known study of the novel, *The Great Tradition*.[2] Alter points to the omission on the part of Leavis of works by such writers as Fielding, Sterne, and Joyce, undoubtedly excluded because of their incompatibility with Leavis' argument for realism as justification for the genre. Alter places the novels of those writers, along with a host of others, from *Don Quixote* to *Tristram Shandy* to the writings of Nabokov, in a "distinctive generic trend"[3] which runs parallel to the great realistic tradition and which he teasingly suggests may be called "the other tradition."

If an artist's expressed awareness of his own art is traceable in the novel to the beginnings of the genre, it is so much more a well-established phenomenon in drama, which, in showing evidence of self-consciousness since its inception, can claim a headstart over the novel of some two thousand years. If any purposeful breaking of the dramatic illusion may be called "self-consciousness," then the chorus of Greek tragedy would represent the earliest extant evidence in Western drama of a playwright's artistic awareness. In the British tradition, medieval drama, not far removed from ritual, is nonillusory. And one of the great eras of world drama, the late sixteenth and early seventeenth centuries in England, offers frequent examples of self-consciousness. Indeed, many of the conventions of the Elizabethan and Jacobean theater, including prologues and epilogues, asides, direct addresses, and the play-within-a-play, are notably self-conscious and, whatever their thematic purpose, exist formally to remind the audience that it is watching a play which, while pretending to be reality, is not.[4]

In early modern drama, it is not uncommon for a character to serve as an authorial spokesman, espousing the philosophical and social ideas of both the fictive character and its creator. And frequently there is a playfulness involved in an author's self-consciousness, as, for example, in *Fanny's First Play* (1910), where Shaw's characters discuss the discussion play Shaw so delighted in creating:

> TROTTER [*emphatically*]: I think I know the sort of entertainments you mean. But please do not beg a vital question by calling them plays . . . these productions, whatever else they may be, are certainly not plays.
> FANNY: The authors dont say they are.
> TROTTER [*warmly*]: I am aware that one author, who is, I blush to say, a personal friend of mine, resorts freely to the dastardly subterfuge of calling them conversations, discussions, and so forth, with the express object of evading criticism. But I'm not to be disarmed by such tricks. I say they are not plays. Dialogues, if you will. Exhibitions of character, perhaps: especially the character of the author. Fictions, possibly. . . . But plays, no. I say NO. Not plays.[5]

Another common example of authorial presence is Thornton Wilder's *Our Town*, where a stage manager presides over the entire production, or *The Skin of Our Teeth*, where Sabina steps out of her role to speak directly to the audience, commenting on her awareness that she is a participant in a play.

But all these instances of disregard for the dramatic illusion are only related to the phenomenon of self-consciousness which characterizes so much modern art. The artistic self-consciousness with which we are concerned here is a persistent and pervasive inward turning which, when pursued to the extreme, results in the form of the work of art becoming the content. The self-conscious art with which we are concerned is supremely aware of itself as artifice and is unabashedly self-reflective. Perhaps the best argument for its justification is Alter's thought-provoking truism, that "literary realism is a tantalizing contradiction in terms."[6] While the great tradition of Western literature willingly accepts fiction as reality, the "other tradition" bases itself on the logical possibility that—since fictions are not real—a work of art comes closer to the truth of reality when it does not pretend to be what it is not, but rather declares itself to be what it is. In fact, Alain Robbe-Grillet, in an essay entitled "From Realism to Reality," makes the point that all revolutions in literature are begun in the name of "realism":

> When a form of writing has lost its initial vitality, its force, its violence, when it has become a vulgar recipe, an academic mannerism which its followers respect only out of routine or laziness, without even questioning its necessity, then it is indeed a return to the real which constitutes the arraignment of the dead formulas and the search for new forms capable of continuing the effort. The discovery of reality will continue only if we abandon outworn forms.[7]

Whether self-conscious art is closer to "reality" than mimetic art is probably an unanswerable question, but it is nonetheless one well worth considering, for self-conscious art may well be modern art's great test of its ontological status.

To imply a distinctively modern quality of self-consciousness, however, is not simply to note the persistent and recurring appearance of self-referentiality within a single work. Indeed, if Lionel Abel is correct in *Metatheatre*, then drama which is pervasively concerned with itself as art is characteristic of the genre since Shakespeare (he particularly notes *Hamlet*), and Alter, studying the novel, points to the phenomenon in full blossom as early as Cervantes. What makes the concept of self-consciousness especially modern is the great outpouring of such works in this century, and particularly since the period between the wars, in virtually every European country and the United States. Indeed, although the realistic tradition is still present (and undoubtedly always will be), its greatness must be shared with the continuous flow of nonmimetic art, art which no longer simply transcribes an external reality but which asserts itself as an autonomous entity, and even, in some cases, *as* reality. Novels from Virginia Woolf to Joyce to Barth and plays from Pirandello to Beckett to Handke, in refusing to be merely passive vehicles for the recording of reality, continue to challenge the great tradition of Western literature.

There is, of course, an explanation for this preponderance of self-conscious art in the modern world. While in formalistic terms it may be viewed as an inevitable reaction against existing forms, self-conscious art is also, and perhaps more importantly, a correlative for the complex intellectual and philosophical temperament of our age. Alter describes our culture as "a kind of Faust at the mirror of Narcissus," which is more and more driven to uncover the roots of what it lives with most basically—language and its origin, human sexuality, the workings of the psyche, the inherited structures of the mind, the underlying patterns of social organization, the sources of value and belief, and, of course, the nature of art.[8]

Our need to know is epitomized, if not perfectly satisfied, by the turning inside out of our own creations, which expose themselves upon probing to the last element of their existence.

Intellectual curiosity, however, is only a symptom (as well as a cause) of the philosophical concerns of the twentieth century which, probably more than ever, are centered on the increasingly difficult-to-define relationship between reality and illusion. Modern man, having experienced the revolutions of Darwin, Freud, and Einstein, as well as the catastrophes of world war, is no longer able to accept the spiritual, moral, and social traditions of the world which he must confront. The absolutes which once informed mankind with a sense of certainty have dissolved into a relativistic vision, relegating reality to a position as subjective as the individual perceptions now believed to create it. Modern man's affirmation of reality has little to do with a metaphysical or even a phenomenal reality; it amounts to an affirmation of the individual consciousness, the subjectivity which Irving Howe, in The Idea of the Modern in Literature and the Arts, has described as "the typical condition of the modernist outlook":

Modernism . . . keeps approaching—sometimes even penetrating—the limits of solipsism, the view expressed by the German poet Gottfried Benn when he writes that "there is no outer reality, there is only human consciousness, constantly building, modifying, rebuilding new worlds out of its own creativity."[9]

In such a world, every man is an artist, for every individual creates his own reality. As R. D. Laing observes in The Politics of Experience:

If there are no meanings, no values, no source of sustenance or help, then man, as creator, must invent, conjure up meanings and values, sustenance and succor out of nothing. He is a magician.[10]

A higher order of "magician" is the artist himself, for he is recording and formalizing his conjurings and offering them to others. Perhaps the burden of responsibility borne by the modern artist is even more serious than that of his predecessors whose task it was to record an external reality, for the artist now is charged with the challenge of "reinvent[ing] the terms of reality."[11] To quote Irving Howe once again, it is the modern artist's "desire to create, or perhaps re-create, the very grounds of being, through a permanent revolution of sensibility and style, by means of which art could raise itself to the level of white or (more likely) black magic."[12] The paradox of modern art, then, is that while the individual consciousness is recognized by modern man as "reality," it is simultaneously recognized as artificer, for it creates reality by interpreting, shaping, and reconstituting the experiences of its perception.

One can readily see how severely the long-existing premise of Western art as an imitation of nature is undercut when one considers that now art and reality, both projections of man's consciousness and both illusion, stand in a radically changed relationship to one another. Indeed, the mere transcription of reality entails a whole new set of standards, for, as Joe David Bellamy asks in his introduction to *Super Fiction*, "If reality becomes surrealistic, what must fiction do to be realistic?"[13] It is not at all surprising, then, that the twentieth century is experiencing—or creating—an aesthetic reevaluation, for it is in art that man finds his most tangible representation of the dialectic between reality and illusion.

The Dramatic Character

Perhaps the best manifestation within a work of art of the relationship between reality and illusion is the fictive character, for in it is embodied the paradox of fiction: the fictive character, like the work of art which contains it, is an artificial reality. Although Jean Valjean, Dorothea Brooke, and Paul Morel may appear to be three-dimensional people, in truth they are composed not of flesh and blood but of words on a printed page. Yet, despite the limits of its existence, the fictive character is a multiplicity of selves. There are as many manifestations of the fictive character as there are perceptions of reality, in that each literary character is the product of an artist's imagination and a reader's imagination as well. And both those imaginations are molded by personal and social preconceptions, as well as those imposed upon the literary creation by the fact that every fictive character has, to some degree, a preexistence in literary tradition. It is this latter fact that informs our response to Augie March, for example, with recollections of Huckleberry Finn, Don Quixote, and Lazarillo de Tormes.

When a fictive character exists in drama, its identity is even more complex. In addition to being an imaginative creation of both author and reader, it also becomes a physical presence functioning before a live audience, which brings to the interpretation not simply the private response of the novel reader, but a collective, communal response as well. Not only does the fictive character take on representational tangibility in drama, but the individual doing the acting also becomes a part of the creative process, presenting and interpreting from yet a third creative mentality. Hence, in terms of components and variables, the dramatic character is the most complex of fictive creations.

Yet it is in its very complexity that the dramatic character asserts its strongest resemblance to the real. One need only consider the complex makeup of a human being to understand how readily the dramatic character may be taken as a metaphor for—if not a rather accurate representation of—the real-life individual. The human being is, of course, a creation of two individuals; though hardly the result of their creative imaginations, he is nonetheless their biological product: they are responsible for his unique genetic makeup. Yet, as in drama, surely this is not what constitutes the "complete" character. The personal attitudes of people with whom the individual interacts are in part responsible for interpreting and forming the individual's character. And social conventions are similarly responsible not only for forming character, but also for endowing the individual with a kind of preexistence, very much like the literary preexistence of Augie March.

Yet there are circumstances under which a dramatic character takes form which are unique to drama. Elizabeth Burns, in
her study *Theatricality*, points to the fact that the special relationship between the audience and the actors is one which does
not exist in real life, where a causal relationship prevails in
human interaction. In the theater, the audience observes characters interacting, but those characters—whose every action, paradoxically, is specifically performed for the sake of the audience—act as though that audience were nonexistent. But the
audience is not simply observer, for, as noted previously, it also
plays a role in the creation of character through its individual
members' preconceptions, attitudes, and responses. Hence there
exists what Burns calls a "double occasion," consisting of "two
distinct but related modes of interaction—interaction between
performers and spectators, and interaction between the characters in the play. . . ." [14]

Burns also points to the fact that in fiction, and particularly
in the theater, "composed" behavior is the norm, whereas in real
life "composed" behavior is equated with role playing for an occasion, a kind of artificial behavior that is distinguished from the
normal, more relaxed behavior of the individual. And lastly, she
points to the fact that fiction, and particularly drama, because it
is so concise and economical, allows certain values to be dis-
played as paradigmatic, whereas they are often obscured by the
diffuseness of life, which does not always make motivation or
cause and effect apparent, as drama does.

The dramatic character is not entirely like his real-life counterpart for another reason, pointed to by Robert Corrigan in "The
Disavowal of Identity in the Modern Theatre." [15] In that essay,
Corrigan reminds us of how persistent a concern identity has
been as a dramatic theme, pointing to Oedipus as the prototype
of the protagonist in search of himself. He notes that in Sophocles' play, the hero finds his identity, an end necessitated by the
nature of classical tragic form. Though aesthetically satisfying,
such an end simply could not be achieved in real life, because in
real life identity is not the fixed entity it is in drama. By definition, identity is a recognizable and unchanging quality, but in
real life man's identity consists of a progression of changing

principles and attitudes that never achieve finality. That a dramatic character is rounded, three-dimensional, or complex does not negate this difference. The fact remains that drama presents a fixed identity, which in real life is a misnomer.

Finally, an important difference between the real-life individual and the dramatic character is the fact that in real life an individual has an existence apart from his actions. Regardless of how complex character is in drama, that character must be expressed through external manifestations. Some of these manifestations may be symbolic, as when fictive characters are endowed with physical characteristics which serve to indicate internal ones, as in Shakespeare's *Richard III*, where the hunchbacked king's deformation is not only physical but moral. Similarly, a character's dress may express something of that character's emotional state, as in *Hamlet*, where dark-colored clothes reflect the grim mood of the young prince. Primarily, though, what the playwright must depend upon as an indicator of character in drama is action (both physical and verbal), the result of the deliberation and decision which Hubert Heffner considers the highest levels of the differentiation which is responsible for dramatic characterization.[16] Despite the tendency of modern literary criticism to celebrate character, Aristotle was surely correct in observing that drama is an "imitation of an action," which means that in drama action precedes character. As Francis Fergusson notes in *The Idea of a Theater*, in drama "we seek to grasp the quality of a man's life, by an imaginative effort, *through* his appearances, his words, and his deeds." And he quotes the words of Virgil in Dante's *Purgatorio*, Canto XVIII, with respect to character: "it is not perceived save in operation, nor manifested except by its effects, as life [is manifested] in a plant by the green leaves."[17]

This is not to say that in real life action is an invalid measure of character, only that it is not a complete measure. A dramatic character is no more than the sum of its actions. As Heffner points out:

> A [dramatic] character is shaped and determined towards a given end; that is, the character is what it is because of its function in a specific kind of action. A playwright assigns qualities and traits to

a character in a play in order to make probable the actions which he must perform in the play and the words which he must say. The function of the character in the whole action determines the traits and characteristics which he must have.[18]

The real-life individual, on the other hand, is not "so teleologically determined":

In the beginning of a human personality the totality of his life cannot be known in the way in which a playwright knows the totality of action which a character must perform in a play.[19]

In real life an individual possesses certain attitudes and values, acquired or innate, that are apart from his actions and which he considers his own unique individuality. Stripped of all the symbolic manifestations of character, a dramatic character (Stanislavsky notwithstanding) is merely an actor, an individual with an identity apart from that of the character he is portraying. In real life, however, the identity established by an individual's actions is only a portion of a total self, which consists also of an individual psychic existence—the character that in real life precedes action.

The modern age has introduced additional complexity into our conception of identity, and in a sense has brought life and drama closer together. In 1917 Pirandello wrote *Right You Are If You Think You Are,* which dramatized the emerging feeling of what Joseph Wood Krutch has called "the dissolution of the ego."[20] Many of the plays which followed, by both Pirandello and others, rendered in dramatic form the fluid nature of the individual identity, the inescapable relativity of man's existence. Now the satisfying end of the search for identity in Sophocles' play, already objectively impossible in life, seemed objectively impossible in drama, for now, even in drama, identity was not a fixed entity. In *Right You Are,* one person, Signora Ponza, is at once Ponza's second wife and Signora Frola's daughter, Ponza's first wife, whom Ponza claims is dead; and we never discover which of the two, mother or husband, is telling the truth, since Signora Ponza herself insists she is both. Individual identity appears dependent upon individual perceptions, and since such perceptions vary among individuals, and even the perceptions of a single individual are inconsistent, so also does the identity of the person or character perceived vary. While the term "dissolution of the ego," as Heffner observes, may itself be ultimately an illusion for Pirandello and hence not an accurate description of the playwright's vision of man,[21] surely Pirandello's plays dramatize (if they do not affirm) the relativity of identity.

An important aspect of this relativity is man's social identity. Man is constantly donning masks in order to play the roles demanded of him, a process for which the theater is a perfect metaphor. Social psychologist Erving Goffman, in fact, in *The Presentation of Self in Everyday Life*, studies the sociology of life in terms of the theatrical metaphor. For Goffman the self is manifested not in the essential being who dons various masks according to social demands, but (as in drama) *through* roles, the roles representing the image of oneself which that person (or the playwright) is trying to convey to others. The theme of role playing becomes a frequent one in modern drama. It is present, for example, in such early plays as Chiarelli's *The Mask and the Face* (1916), where Paolo, the cuckolded husband, is perplexed by the fact that when he was thought a murderer he was not jailed, but when he is discovered *not* to be one, he is threatened with imprisonment and must leave his home and begin a life of disguise; Pirandello's *The Rules of the Game* (1918), where Leone responds to life as a game, acting his part with calculated precision, and forcing his wife's lover, Guido, to play his; and O'Neill's *The Great God Brown* (1925), where a theatrical mask is placed on the face of Dion Anthony to symbolize the outward character, which his wife and others know, as opposed to the inward character, the unmasked face of which frightens Margaret. The dramatization of the rift between the outward or social self and the inward or real self intensifies the question as to whether the phenomenon of role playing has become so significant in the modern world that the prayer of the real-life individual, like that of Tom Stoppard's Guildenstern, is "Give us this day our daily mask,"[22] for he is identifiable only in terms of his roles.

Edmund Fuller, in *Man in Modern Fiction*, argues (from a

Christian viewpoint) that man has become morally answerable only to social contracts. Modern man is "collective, irresponsible, morally neuter, and beyond help."[23] Robert Corrigan, in "The Transformation of the Individual in the Modern Theatre," argues (from a Marxian viewpoint) that modern man has become a functional being. Industrialization, he suggests, has resulted in so high a degree of specialization that only an individual's "specific technical abilities" matter.[24] If collectivism and its consequences have progressed to the point where an essential self no longer exists, then the relationship between the fictive character and the real-life individual must be reconsidered. If identity is defined in life in terms of actions or roles and modern man's essential self is denied, then the traditional dramatic character, itself no more than the sum of its actions, is closer to being an exact representation of its real-life counterpart than it ever has been.

Or does modern man, as C. C. Walcutt suggests, "reject the suggestion that people are only what they do, for we must believe that they absolutely and essentially *are* something whether they do anything or not"?[25] Does man still possess what Joseph Wood Krutch defends as an essential self?[26] If this is the case, then we may look to modern drama for a reflection of modern man's stubborn insistence upon the integrity of the individual apart from his roles. We may look to those playwrights who reject the condition of social roles as a final statement of human identity for an affirmation of the real identity behind the fictive identity in real life. Either way, modern drama is abundantly informed with a commitment to examining the relationship between the "real" and the "role" in human identity, a commitment which is integrally involved with the problematic relationship of reality and fiction in both philosophic and artistic terms. It is in the metafictional character that these concerns find common ground.

The Metafictional Character

By its very nature, the dramatic character is twofold: it is simultaneously both actor and character. While we are intellectually
aware of this duality, our submission to the dramatic illusion
requires a suspension of our knowledge that a real individual
other than the character being portrayed is before us. Normally
we willingly accept this convention. In the plays which are the
subject of this study, however, the playwrights have not made
this traditional demand upon us, and in asking us *not* to forget
the fictive nature of the *dramatis personae*, have instead created
a situation which may be more demanding intellectually and
confusing emotionally, but which ultimately is truer to the conception of drama than the conventional absorption in illusion.
For by insisting that the audience cognitively maintain bifocal
vision, the playwright is constantly and overtly sustaining the
dialectic which exists between reality and illusion.

Genet is among the more blatant enforcers of the conception
of revealing rather than concealing the fictional nature of his
characters. In *Our Lady of the Flowers*, for example, he speaks of
a contrast between actor and character which he might later have
hoped to see employed in *The Maids*:

> If I were to have a play put on in which women had roles, I would
> insist that these roles be performed by adolescent boys, and I
> would so inform the audience by means of a placard which would
> remain nailed to the right or left of the set throughout the perfor-
> mance.[27]

A less obvious but equally appropriate example is Beckett's
Waiting for Godot, in which the playwright never allows his audience to lose sight of the fact that his protagonists are not only
Didi and Gogo, the tramps waiting for the arrival of Godot, but
actors as well.

The result in the Genet and Beckett plays, and in scores of
other modern plays, of a playwright's calling attention to the
actor *qua* actor is an awareness on the part of the audience of the
similarity between the real-life individual and the dramatic char-

acter. For in emphasizing the rift between the essential self (the actor) and the role-playing self (the character), the playwright immediately suggests the loss of identity experienced by modern man as well as a sense of the artificiality of theater and the essentially dramatic quality of life. The moment an individual assumes a social role, a duality materializes which is precisely the duality that is inherently present in the dramatic character: an actor, "mask[ing] his internal self,"[28] creates a role and becomes a character. By virtue of the physical presence of the actor, then, any single character in drama (unlike his counterpart in the novel) is inherently dualistic.

The duality which is inherent in any dramatic character and in the dramatic event is at the heart of the metafictional character we are examining here. For that duality, when manifested as a twofoldness in the fictive character itself, results in the simultaneous separation and coalescence of reality and illusion and a heightened awareness of the fact that the two dimensions, the real and the fictive, exist in both the theater and life. The metafictional character, whether he be game-playing, role-playing, or involved in any number of variations, possesses two distinct fictive identities, between which we are forced to distinguish, accepting one of the fictive identities as "real" and the other as "fictive." At times the metafictional character is the embodiment of one portion of its duality, and at other times the embodiment of the other portion. Ultimately, though, these two aspects of reality and illusion are both embodied in the same character, giving the playwright the perfect opportunity to confuse them once he has distinguished them. The metafictional character, then, goes beyond the traditional role of the character, maintaining its pretense of reality yet vigorously asserting its own fictive existence, and in its duality serving as metaphor for the compelling concerns of the modern artist.

Among the earliest metafictional characters in modern drama are those in Michel de Ghelderode's *The Death of Doctor Faust*. The epigraph to this study, in fact, is a passage from that play and is perhaps the most succinct definition of the metafictional character:

Then tell me where is Faust?
Where does he begin? Where does he end?
Is he a fiction? . . .
He is real and false at the same time.[29]

While the coalescence of reality and illusion is not physically realized within one character in *Doctor Faust* until the death of (the) Doctor(s) Faust, the duality with which later playwrights are so concerned is clearly embodied in the two Fausts through the expressed awareness of theatricality. Ghelderode calls the play a "drama of identity," in which the sixteenth-century Faust experiences a "displacement of the personality"[30] and sets out to find himself. The quest entails a transplantation of the philosopher into the twentieth century and a physical split between the acting self (which Faust is determined to reject) and the real self (which Faust is determined to find). Each of the play's three central characters—Faust, Marguerite, and Diamotoruscant (the devil)—has a counterpart who is, respectively, the Actor Faust, the Actress Marguerite, and the Actor Devil. As these actors perform in a tavern, the real characters assume the position of audience, underscoring Ghelderode's awareness of the essentially dramatic quality of life.

But the detachment does not survive the play. When Faust seduces Marguerite, the Actor Faust finds himself responsible for Faust's actions and, much to his own confusion, seeks refuge in the world of the sixteenth-century Faust. When the two Fausts meet there, they argue over who is the "real" Faust, Faust contending that he is the true one since he is "the ancient one," and the Actor Faust contending he is the true one since he is Faust "in the eyes of a crowd."[31] Although Faust had earlier complained of the falsity of his character, he now belatedly discovers that when the Actor Faust is killed, he too must be destroyed, for it is only in the simultaneous presence of the fictive and the real that the character can exist. Doctor Faust, along with all dramatic characters and, indeed, real-life individuals as well, is essentially both fictive and real.

Pirandello's *Six Characters*, of course, precedes Ghelderode's *Doctor Faust*, and Chiarelli's *The Mask and the Face* precedes

Six Characters. But in this case it is far more appropriate to look forward from the twenties rather than backward, for drama since World War II has been persistently characterized by the presence of such metafictional characters. The importance of Pirandello, however, cannot be overstated, and because of his seminal position in the establishment of modern drama in the self-conscious tradition, a chapter is devoted to Henry IV, who, in his possession of both a mad (or fictive) identity as the eleventh-century king and a sane (or real) identity as the unnamed young man who loved Donna Matilda, may well be called the prototype of the metafictional character.

Except for the characters of Pirandello, the fictive beings discussed here are all the products of the post-World-War-II years. Representing the contemporary phenomenon of the metafictional character are Genet's sisters in The Maids, his brothel patrons in The Balcony, and his white-black court characters in The Blacks, all of which get at reality through fantasy worlds; Beckett's game-playing tramps of Waiting for Godot and playacting couple of Endgame; the asylum inmates in Weiss's Marat/Sade; Albee's Martha and George, in Who's Afraid of Virginia Woolf?, who create an alternate existence for themselves as imaginary parents; Rosencrantz and Guildenstern, minor characters in Hamlet, but the protagonists of Stoppard's play, and Moon and Birdboot, the critic-actors of The Real Inspector Hound.

The arrangement of characters in this study is roughly chronological. No development is suggested among the playwrights by virtue of chronology, though collectively their plays do represent an historical development in the conception and rendering of dramatic art. There is a purposeful heterogeneity in terms of national origin (an Italian, a Frenchman, an Irishman living in France, a German living in Sweden, an American, and a Czech living in England), which may suggest the pervasiveness of the phenomenon of self-consciousness and the metafictional character in modern drama. As a postscript to this study, a chapter is devoted to Peter Handke. In his case, a development is suggested, for this difficult and unconventional Austrian (living in France) playwright, while not the creator of a metafictional character as it is defined in this study, displays an undeniable awareness of the specific duality out of which that character has grown and consciously eliminates that duality rather than emphasizing it. And his play, *The Ride Across Lake Constance,* in its virtually total self-sufficiency as art, seems a fitting close to this study of "the other tradition."

It is not the purpose of the present work to catalogue systematically each of the playwright's references to the play as play, the theater as theater, or art as art, or to collect all the instances of overt theatricality or play-life metaphors. Rather, this study will examine the creation and function of one reappearing dramatic outgrowth of the inexhaustible catalogue of self-consciousness in modern drama: the metafictional character.

✠One
Pirandello's Henry IV

TO SAY THAT self-conscious modern drama began with Pirandello would be like saying that realism began with Balzac, naturalism with Zola, or surrealism with Breton: all of these are oversimplifications that wrongly imply a literary concept is the pure product of one man's genius rather than the outgrowth of a complex combination of prevailing values and attitudes—and the need to find expression for those values and attitudes— which are the temper and ripeness of a particular era. Pirandello was not alone in his dramatic achievement, nor was he even the first. Indeed, it is ultimately impossible to fix with exactness the first modern dramatic rendering of the "other tradition." Depending on one's specific criteria, any one of a number of playwrights—Ibsen, Chekhov, Shaw, Zola, Maeterlinck, Strindberg, Jarry, Apollinaire, Chiarelli, Schnitzler, and several others— might qualify as being the playwright of seminal importance. Yet it is not difficult to understand why the phrase "after Pirandello" has become a critical commonplace, for, as Francis Fergusson notes in *The Idea of a Theater*, Pirandello is symbolically, if not chronologically, the point at which a new form of drama emerged.[1]

In the early 1920s, the plays of Pirandello were performed in New York, London, Paris, Berlin, and Vienna, as well as in Pirandello's native Italy.[2] Possibly the strongest and most immediate impact of the playwright was felt in France, where the 1923 production of *Six Characters in Search of an Author* at the Comédie des Champs-Elysées in Paris greatly excited the critics. Henri Beraud, for example, acclaimed the play as having "overwhelmed my soul," and Pierre Brisson called it "a new achievement in the contemporary history of the theater."[3] It was this play about which Georges Neveux would later remark: "The entire theatre of an era came out of the womb of the play, *Six Characters*."[4] Within two years, the Sicilian's reputation secure, Pirandello's plays were "everywhere":

> at the Atelier, at the Renaissance, at the Théâtre des Arts; he is being played in three theaters at the same time—a fact without precedent for a foreign author; it's a rage, an infatuation, a fancy, a craze.[5]

In 1926, Gaston Rageot christened Pirandello "the great dramatist of the western world."[6] Nor was the playwright's significance to diminish. In his 1947 study of the French theater, Marcel Doisy testifies to Pirandello's continuing impact:

> Surely no man of the theater since Ibsen had given Europe so totally renewed conceptions of the theater, a more violently original artistry together with so personal a technique. . . . And it certainly seems as if his revelations are still far from being exhausted. . . . Pirandello might easily remain one of the guiding lights of the period which is opening.[7]

The canon of Pirandellian drama is like a symphony, stating and restating, embellishing, varying a single theme. Virtually all of Pirandello's plays reflect the artist's nearly obsessive preoccupation with the relationship between reality and illusion, be it with respect to the philosophical conception of the relativity of truth, the fluid and multiple nature of the personality, or the persistent division between life and art. In his rendering of the multiplicity of identity, the playwright, undoubtedly influenced by the *teatro del grotesco*, repeatedly distinguishes between the "mask," which all of us assume, and the "face," which constantly remains veiled. In his inquiry into the relativity of truth, he constructs and demolishes layers of illusion, probing into the multiple perceptions and identities of his characters to reveal yet conceal the "naked mask." In his fascination with his own power as artist-creator, he dramatizes the dialectic between the fluid, spontaneous, sprawling nature of life and the fixed, predictable and contained nature of art. But as Robert Brustein points out in *The Theatre of Revolt*, the areas of Pirandello's dramatic inquiry are all facets of the same subject:

> The typical Pirandellian drama is a drama of frustration which has at its core an irreconcilable conflict between time and timelessness or life and form; and whether the author is reflecting on human identity or (his other major subject) the identity of art, the terms of the conflict remain essentially the same.[8]

For Pirandello, the metafictional character is the dramatic embodiment of this multiple single theme.

Because Pirandello is so concerned with the nature of identity, nearly every one of his major characters (Signora Ponza in *Right You Are* or Leone in *Rules of the Game*, for example) possesses a "mask" as well as a "face." And because he is so concerned with the nature of theater, many (such as the characters in *Each in His Own Way* or *Tonight We Improvise*) also possess an expressed awareness of their identities as actors. In fact, most of Pirandello's characters may be called metafictional characters, for whether their acting role is psychological or social on the one hand, or theatrical on the other—or both—they serve as symbols of the playwright's concern with the multiple facets of the relationship between reality and illusion.

One Pirandellian character in particular may well be called the prototype of the metafictional character in modern self-conscious drama, and that is the protagonist of *Henry IV*. As Brustein perceives:

> In Henry's character, Pirandello's reflections on the conflict between life and form, on the elusiveness of identity, and on man's revolt against time, achieve their consummation. . . . Henry is the culmination of Pirandello's notions (developed more elaborately in his theatre plays) about the timeless world of art.[9]

In terms of its presentation of the complexity of identity, *Henry IV* (1922) is perhaps the richest of the Pirandello canon. No character in that play exists singularly as a fictive creation, but each moves from one self to another as the action shifts from the distant past to the recent past to the present. Donna Matilda, the protagonist's former love, possesses no fewer than five identities: she is at once the middle-aged Donna Matilda of the present; the masked Donna Matilda of twenty years earlier; the Marchioness Matilda of Tuscany of eight hundred years earlier; the Duchess Adelaide, mother of Empress Bertha of Susa, who was the historical eleventh-century king's wife; and, through her daughter, the youthful Donna Matilda chronologically misplaced. Which of these several selves she is at a given moment is dependent upon the role she voluntarily assumes (as when she pretends, upon first seeing the "madman," to be Adelaide), or, more commonly, the identity imposed upon her by the protagonist. That character's perceptions, depending on whether they emanate from the eleventh-century king, the love-struck young man of twenty years earlier, or the middle-aged man of the present, permit Donna Matilda to move through a twenty-year time span of reality and an eight-hundred-year time span of fantasy, and to be several selves simultaneously. The central symbol of this fluidity and multiplicity of identity is the masquerade: the protagonist's delusions began at a masquerade pageant; Donna Matilda is masquerading as a character from both the protagonist's past and Henry IV's past; those in the group of characters who visit the castle are donning masks which conceal the face in the ultimate hope of revealing the face of the protagonist, who is the master masquerader.

Even with this multiplicity of selves, however, there exists a basic duality which creates the metafictional character. Every character in Henry IV possesses a double identity within the fictive world; every character, already fictive, plays the part of a fictive character in the fiction within the fictive world of the play. In the face of such role playing within role playing, we are forced to differentiate between the two fictive roles, one of which we accept as the "real" fictive character. Thus we have the young men who cater to Henry's whims possessing one identity when they talk among themselves, use electric lights, and smoke cigarettes, and another identity when they are in the presence of the eleventh-century monarch. Similarly, the throne room guests who hope to cure the would-be king are "real" in their capacities as former love, her lover and her daughter, the nephew, and the doctor; they are fictive when they wear the masks of personages from the past of the historical Henry. The double identities of all the characters in the play, however, are dependent upon the double identity of the central character, the man who believes—and does not believe—himself to be Henry IV, king of the Holy Roman Empire.

Before looking at the duality of the protagonist of *Henry IV*, however, it might be appropriate to examine the dialectic which is responsible for creating the character which belongs to both the world of fiction and the world of reality, and to that end turn to another Pirandellian play, which was written one year earlier than *Henry IV*, and is somewhat less developed in terms of this concept. For in *Six Characters* (1921), two groups—the Characters and the Actors—rather than a single character, embody the two fictive identities. Our response therefore (or at least our initial response) is comfortably divided; since it is a *donnée* of the play that we do not accept the fictive creations (i.e., Characters and Actors) equally, we must imaginatively endow one group with the status of "real." We readily choose the Actors—a group of men and women realistically rehearsing a play when we happened upon them—and remind oursleves of the premise of drama involving the creation of any dramatic character: the actor, of course, is real; the character, fictive. Even though the premise is not so simply applied here, since in this case the Actors are no more real than the Characters (they, too, are fictive creations being played by real people), their juxtaposition with the Characters, who are, by self-admission, fictive, authenticates their reality.

Initially, then, there is no problem in isolating reality from illusion. Six Characters appear on stage during a rehearsal of a Pirandello play and declare themselves to be the products of an author's imagination, an author who has created but abandoned them. Their intrusion upon the world of the Actors readily allows us to establish the dichotomy of fictive (the Characters) and "real" (the Actors). Gradually, however, Pirandello (predictably) upsets this distinction.

The Characters, who wish only to be immortalized through the written text, insist upon their autonomy, claiming an existence independent of the play which attempts to portray them. They find that the Actors cannot portray them with fidelity, for the Actors themselves interpret and create, making of the Characters something quite different from what the Characters claim is their true identity. The Characters want only fidelity to what they know as their own experience, but cannot find it in the reflection of art. They enact (or re-experience) their tragic story and then watch the Actors imperfectly perform the same scene. We soon find that the failure of the Actors to record accurately the experience of the Characters lends a validity to the Characters, upsetting our earlier delegation of them to the world of illusion and of the Actors to the world of reality.

Yet the characters do not claim reality; they reaffirm the fact that they are illusion:

> THE FATHER: Now . . . , if you consider the fact that we . . . as we are, have no other reality outside of this illusion . . .
> THE MANAGER: . . . And what does that mean?
> THE FATHER: . . . As I say, sir, that which is a game of art for you is our sole reality.[10]

The audience must now adjust its thinking to include the possibility that illusion is more real than reality, particularly since the Characters retain their identities irrespective of time. As the father questions the manager's identity, asking him who he is and pointing to his changing reality, the present being "fated to seem a mere illusion"[11] tomorrow, we add to our thinking the further possibility that perhaps reality *is* illusion. The Characters, who have no reality beyond the illusion, are thus as real as the "real" individual whose identity is an illusive one. Through the exploitation of the dichotomy between the real and the fictive, Pirandello has dramatized several concerns: the fluidity of identity, the philosophic relationship of reality and illusion, and the relationship of life and art.

Yet one character does not embody the dichotomy of the real and the fictive. In *Six Characters* it is simply a case of our being manipulated into viewing a given set of characters as "real" and then as fictive, and vice versa, to dramatize that dichotomy. The principle with which we are concerned here is intact, but we must look ahead to *Henry IV* for the single metafictional character which is "real and false at the same time."

When *Henry IV* opens, Berthold, a newcomer to the castle, is being initiated into the routine of an attendant of Henry IV. Having believed the madman to be the "other" Henry IV, the sixteenth-century king of France, Berthold is in frantic need of background details, which the other attendants gladly supply (and which Pirandello obliges us with as well). The man who believes himself to be Henry IV has been acting the role for some twenty years. Two decades earlier, dressed as the eleventh-century king at a masquerade pageant, and youthfully in love with Donna Matilda, herself dressed as Matilda of Tuscany, Henry's historical enemy, the protagonist was thrown from his horse and became fixated in the identity of the mask he wore. Donna Matilda describes the tragic event:

> I shall never forget that scene—all our masked faces hideous and terrified gazing at him, at that terrible mask of his face, which was no longer a mask, but madness, madness personified.[12]

We and the attendants soon learn, however, that the madman recovered from the fixation eight years earlier, but, choosing not to return to the real world from which he had been absent for twelve years, hid his lucidity and continued the illusion of his delusion.

The double existence of the protagonist in *Henry IV*, then, is manifested, on the one hand, in the "real" self, the man (whose name we never learn) who twenty years earlier was enamoured of Donna Matilda, dressed the part of Henry IV, and, twelve years after that, consciously regained his identity but did not reveal this fact to others. On the other hand, it is manifested in the fictive self, that of the eleventh-century king of the Holy Roman Empire, which for twelve years was the result of the madness of the protagonist and for eight years the result of his "lucid madness." For eight years, then, there has been an overlapping of the "real" and the fictive selves, for while Henry was unaware of his masquerade at first, he is now, and has been for eight years, supremely aware of it, yet persists in maintaining it.

Translated into social terms, Henry is an extreme example of the individual who as social animal adopts roles in order to fulfill the image others have of him. Yet there is a strange superiority in the kind of role playing to which the protagonist is committed as compared with the kind of role playing in which the social individual—and the castle guests and valets—indulge. When he is actually mad, the protagonist is playing a role in earnest; he is so totally committed to his identity as Henry that any distinction existing between fiction and reality dissolves, inextricably merging, at least for Henry, the mask and the face. When he is lucidly mad, though, he is playing the role in full consciousness that it is an illusion, but his madness is being sustained not in deference to any demands of society, but for his own purposes: first, because he is psychologically unable to rejoin a world from which he has been absent for twelve years, and secondly, for his own amusement. For eight years the protagonist has been in complete command of his role and in partial command of those of others, which he creates and manipulates in relation to his own. By contrast, the make-believe of the castle guests and the valets is one which is created exclusively for the benefit of Henry. Recognizing them as fools, Henry can chide the valets for not having "known how to create a fantasy for yourselves, not to act it for me" (p. 194).

On a psychological level, Henry is also superior, for he is the only one who can believe "the moon in the pond is real" (p. 193). The others, rigidly fixed in a concept of themselves, are incapable of simultaneously believing and not believing the lie. Where Henry dyes his hair for a joke, the Marchioness does it seriously in an effort to fulfill her own static image of herself. But Henry tells his former love:

> I assure you that you too, Madam, are in masquerade, though it be in all seriousness; and I am not speaking of the venerable crown

on your brows or the ducal mantle. I am speaking only of the
memory you wish to fix in yourself of your fair complexion one
day when it pleased you. . . .   (p. 170)

Henry alone possesses what Doctor Dionysius Genoni characterizes as "the peculiar psychology of madmen; . . . [he can] detect
people who are disguised; . . . recognize the disguise and yet
believe in it; . . . [and he can understand that] disguise is both
play and reality" (p. 174). Only the protagonist can "act the madman to perfection":

> and I do it very quietly, I'm only sorry for you that you have to
> live your madness so agitatedly, without knowing it or seeing it.
>   (pp. 205–6)

The protagonist's duality may exist in terms of identity, in
both social and psychological terms, and indeed it may offer a
perspective on social roles and the psychological concept of self,
but it is surely not limited to that concern in this play (or, for
that matter, in any of the other plays in this study).

Pirandello's other great subject is the relationship between
life and art, and the protagonist's duality is well worth considering in aesthetic terms. If the middle-aged protagonist is the
"real" self and the eleventh-century king the fictive self, then we
may also equate the division of sanity and madness ("madness,"
"fantasy," "unreality," "illusion" all suggesting creative genius
and the product of that genius) and the division of life and art.
From the psychological crisis of the protagonist, then, emerges a
metaphor not only for the self in its social and psychological
manifestations, but for the play itself, through which the playwright may examine the validity of art in the face of an uncertain
reality.

The distinction that exists between life and art has long been
a concern of literary creators, especially so among modern
writers. In his 1889 essay, "The Decay of Lying," Oscar Wilde,
through the voice of his fictive Vivian, proclaims the superiority
of art:

> My own experience is that the more we study Art, the less we care
> for Nature. What Art really reveals to us is Nature's lack of design,
> her curious crudities, her extraordinary monotony, her absolutely

unfinished condition. Nature has good intentions, of course, but, as Aristotle once said, she cannot carry them out. When I look at a landscape I cannot help seeing all its defects. It is fortunate for us, however, that Nature is so imperfect, as otherwise we should have no art at all. Art is our spirited protest, our gallant attempt to teach Nature her proper place.[13]

In his inquiry into the relationship of reality and illusion in *Henry IV*, Pirandello focuses particularly on an aspect of art existing as part of the orderliness suggested by Vivian and clearly distinguishing it from reality, and that is timelessness.

Like the characters in *Six Characters*, man, a temporal creature, is constantly seeking relief from the flux of existence, a means of freezing what Pirandello, in his 1920 essay, *On Humor*, calls "the continuous flow":

> Life is a continuous flow which we continually try to stop, to fix in established and determinate forms outside and inside of ourselves because we are already fixed forms, forms that move among other immovable ones, which follow the flow of life until the point when they become rigid and their movement, slowed, stops.

The means by which we attempt to achieve permanence is illusion:

> The forms in which we try to stop and fix this continuous flow are the concepts, the ideals, within which we want to keep coherent all the fictions we create, the condition and the status in which we try to establish ourselves.[14]

For twelve years Henry was the realization of this striving; he had succeeded in suspending his susceptibility to the "poisonous ingenuity of time" which Beckett describes in *Proust*: "There is no escape from the hours and the days. Neither from to-morrow nor from yesterday."[15] While *chronos* continued on its course, Henry remained the young king of Germany, reliving the events of a concentrated period of time from 1076, when the historical king penitently knelt before Pope Gregory VII, to 1080, when he was supreme ruler over the entire empire, including the pope.[16] For Henry, immovably fixed in history, the past, present, and future were a concentrated and constant reality.

For eight years, however, the protagonist has been only pretending to be Henry IV. Within his self-created fiction, he—or at least his mask—is still immune from time, a delusion which the others, by responding to him as though he were Henry, support. For the protagonist himself, however, his susceptibility to time is the one certainty of his sanity. He may yet dress as Henry IV and "relive" the events of the eleventh century, but for eight years he has been aware of his own greying hair and of the absence of much of a resemblance between the portrait of the youthful man dressed as Henry IV and the middle-aged man his mirror reflects. The fact is that while the fictive side of the protagonist's double existence has remained fixed, the "real" side has moved irretrievably forward in time.

It is not difficult to see the emerging metaphor of life and art in the protagonist's dual nature. Life, which is subject to time, is a progression of haphazard events, none of which can be relived. Art, which transcends time, freezes events into a permanent, repeatable pattern. The unnamed protagonist, then, who frets over his greying reflection, is the embodiment of life. Henry, the other part of the double character, in his immunity from time, his capacity to relive events in the past as a present reality, his ability to give permanence to illusion, is the embodiment of the spirit and function of art.

The relationship between art and reality which is embodied in Pirandello's central character is externally symbolized by the portraits of Donna Matilda and the youthful protagonist which hang on the wall of the throne room. Originally, these portraits, which reflected the young couple in their masquerade pageant costumes, were thought by the protagonist to be images; when he regained his sanity and became aware of his own temporality, he preserved the portraits as a means of fostering the youthful image he knew no longer was fact. The portraits, after all, as art, possessed the very quality of permanence of Henry's madness:

> A portrait is always there fixed in the twinkling of an eye: it can bring back everything: movement, gestures, looks, smiles, a whole heap of things. (p. 152)

But the portraits, once reflectors of reality and now betrayers of it, soon become reality. Like the portrait in Oscar Wilde's novel, they become "animated inanimate duplicates,"[17] but to an even greater degree than in the portrait of Dorian Gray, which ages within its frame. Here the portraits, replaced by Donna Matilda's daughter and the protagonist's nephew, emerge from the frames which enclose them and assume living form. Just as the young protagonist had twenty years earlier become the realization of an illusion, so the portraits are no longer art, but reality.

The doctor's plan was to present the protagonist with a double image—the youthful couple and the aged couple—in hopes of telescoping time and shocking the madman into sanity. But because the protagonist is already cured *before* the shock treatment, the performance is a perilous one: the portraits are acquiring life before a man who finds security in the fact that his real self is indeed subject to time. For the madman, perceiving the live forms of Donna Matilda (actually her daughter) and himself (actually his nephew) as they were twenty years earlier and, immediately after, the live forms of the present Donna Matilda and himself, might have resulted in the restoration of his personality. But for the man whose sanity rests so seriously on his awareness of time as a continuum, a perception now seriously disturbed, the reincarnation could just as readily result in convincing the protagonist that he is the eleventh-century king. In fact, the treatment is abruptly discontinued when the others enter the throne room to announce their discovery that Henry is already cured. The face before them now is no longer that of Henry IV; it is the "naked mask."

And it is as the naked mask that the protagonist responds, embracing Frida as his youthful love Matilda, joyfully pouring forth twenty years of suppressed emotion. But he is embracing Frida for an even more important reason: the young woman, once frozen in form, is now pure life. It is this spontaneity and freedom which he so enthusiastically, almost frenetically, embraces, only to be thought a madman for doing so.

Seeing the impossibility of life without illusion, and without love, the protagonist must return to the mask of his madness, where illusion is tolerated and love is an eternal force. He cries his torment, which "is really this: that whether here or there [Pointing to his portrait . . .] I can't free myself from this magic" (p. 172). By slaying Belcredi, he permanently seals himself in the "eternal masquerade." As the dying man is carried offstage crying, "No, no, you're not mad! You're not mad. He's not mad!" (p. 208)—a sentiment not shared by the others—the protagonist, "with the most lucid consciousness" (p. 204), slips permanently into the role of Henry IV.

Admirers and detractors of Pirandello alike have long commented on the playwright's incessant hammering away at the theme of reality and illusion. The playwright himself in fact playfully comments on his own endless preoccupation in *Each In His Own Way* (1924), where, in an interlude in which the first act is criticized by defenders and opponents of Pirandello, a spectator complains: "But why is he always harping on this illusion and reality string?" (p. 317). The aspect of the relationship of reality and illusion which presents itself most readily to readers of Pirandello's plays is that of relativity. But the playwright's preoccupation extends considerably beyond the dramatization of the way in which we "simulate and dissimulate with ourselves, splitting or even multiplying ourselves,"[18] to the central philosophical question underlying all his drama: exactly what the relationship between reality and illusion consists of.

In a 1923 essay which shows considerable sensitivity to Pirandello's philosophy, Adriano Tilgher discusses the dialectic of life and form which is at the core of virtually every essay, short story, and play the Sicilian wrote. Tilgher observes that man is unique among living things in possessing consciousness of life. Unlike a tree, which is "completely immersed in its own vital sense,"[19] not distinguishing itself from its environment, man possesses both life and the feeling of life. This unique consciousness, detaching itself from life, creates a new life of forms—"the concepts and ideals of our spirit, the conventions, mores, traditions and laws of society."[20] These forms, however, conflict with the free flow of life, imprisoning man within their molds, and, finally, replacing life as the only seeming reality.

Robert Brustein, discussing the affinities of Pirandello and Bergson, similarly summarizes this relationship, characterizing the playwright's concept of life:

> Life (or reality or time) is fluid, mobile, evanescent, and indeterminate. It lies beyond the reach of reason, and is reflected only through spontaneous action, or instinct. Yet man, endowed with reason, cannot live instinctually like the beasts, nor can he accept an existence which constantly changes. In consequence, he uses reason to fix life through ordering definitions. Since life is indefinable, such concepts are illusions. Man is occasionally aware of the illusory nature of his concepts; but to be human is to desire form; anything formless fills man with dread and uncertainty.[21]

And Pirandello himself describes the conflict in *On Humor:*

> All phenomena either are illusory or their reason escapes us inexplicably. Our knowledge of the world and of ourselves refuses to be given the objective value which we usually attempt to attribute to it. Reality is a continuously illusory construction. The obstacles and the limitations we place upon our consciousness are also illusions. They are the conditions of the appearance of our relative individuality. In reality, these limitations do not exist.[22]

Art, then, and all of man's illusions, are created in response to this dialectic. And their absolute necessity is understood perhaps most immediately in the novel, *The Late Mattia Pascal,* which Tilgher describes:

> To enjoy life in its infinite nakedness and freedom, outside all constructed forms into which society, history, and the events of each individual existence have channeled its course, is impossible. Mattia Pascal tried that, who, palming himself off as dead and changing name and aspect, believed he could start a new life, in the enthusiasm of a boundless liberty. He learned at his own expense that, having cut himself off from all social forms and conventions, he was only allowed to witness other people's life as a foreign spectator, without any further possibility to mingle with it and enjoy its fullness. Since he had estranged himself from the forms of life, it now no longer conceded itself to him except superficially, externally.[23]

The experience of Henry IV is a similar one of alienation. But in his case, the would-be king has cut himself off from both life and the forms others lived by, creating a unique form of his own which enabled him totally to live his illusion. And when, like

Pascal, he attempted, if only for a moment, an affirmation of pure life without form, he was branded as a madman. Neither achieved the balance of life and form which Pirandello believes is the wisdom of life and which Tilgher so appropriately describes:

> To accept the Forms or constructions into which Life has been forced; to participate in them with heartful belief and yet avoid crystallizing oneself in one of them or in one of their systems, but to retain so much spiritual fusion or fluidity that one's soul may go on from form to form without finally coagulating in any, without fearing the impurities it inevitably carries along in its ceaseless flow, since that very flowing will purify it: here is the practical wisdom of life.[24]

The protagonist's retreat into illusion, then, is not a denial of an absolute reality in deference to twentieth-century relativism, but rather an affirmation of the unceasing interdependence of reality and illusion, of life and form, which must characterize life if man is to make any sense of a reality of which he sees only the shadow.

Illusion, then, is not only a competing force simultaneously reflecting and contradicting reality; it is a necessity, for it constitutes the only reality mankind is capable of perceiving and affirms man's constant need for form. And art offers us a packaged epitome of the "magic" from which Henry and we cannot escape, within the fictionalized reality that is its world. In 1920 Pirandello spoke of his feelings about his art:

> I think that life is a very sad piece of buffoonery; because we have in ourselves, without being able to know why, wherefore or whence, the need to deceive ourselves constantly by creating a reality (one for each and never the same for all), which from time to time is discovered to be vain and illusory. . . . My art is full of bitter compassion for all those who deceive themselves; but this compassion cannot fail to be followed by the ferocious derision of destiny which condemns man to deception.[25]

For Pirandello, art is a redeeming force through which man preserves the illusion which must eternally coexist with reality, and a purgative for the constant frustration of man's final inability to know. And the double character is the distillation of the dialectic between life and form, reality and illusion, that is the play-wright's single theme.

After the dissections, demolitions, and restructurings of reality which have taken place over the past two decades at the hands of such playwrights as Beckett, Ionesco, Stoppard, and Handke, the blatantly manipulative plays of Pirandello may no longer seem the fascinating inquiries into the nature of illusion and reality they once were, but may now appear to be naive and rather tiresome belaborings of a theme treated by others in more sophisticated ways. Yet Pirandello's creation of the metafictional character in *Henry IV* must remain the prototype for modern drama, for through it he has perfectly distilled the dialectic between life and form, reality and illusion, that is his own and the modern playwright's recurring theme.

❧Two
Genet's Maids, Brothel Patrons, and Blacks

THE POSTWAR ERA in France was a tremendously prolific one for drama. While plays were still produced during the German occupation, the liberation of 1944 brought with it the rejuvenation of a theater waiting to find expression. The pessimistic spirit and existential anguish which characterized the defeat of France filtered into much of the drama, manifesting itself in the works of the "existentialists" (such as Sartre and Camus) and the "absurdists" (such as Adamov, Beckett, and Ionesco). The new theater of France—those "pocket theater" plays that were not standard Boulevard or Comédie-Française fare—thrived on experimentation, making France perhaps the most significant contributor to the emergence of contemporary drama.

Among the young French avant-garde dramatists of the late 1940s and the 1950s was Jean Genet. Undoubtedly affected by the temper of the age, Genet was the product as well of a personal injustice. Born an unwanted child, Genet was a social outcast—later an anarchist—and spent much of his life in reform schools and prisons. His literary career began in one such prison in 1944 when, at the age of thirty-four, he wrote the novel *Our Lady of the Flowers*. Several years later, the now established but still criminal writer turned to drama, producing five full-length plays.

As the style and vision of the dramatist developed, his affinity with Antonin Artaud (whom he may not actually have read until late in his career) became clear. Artaud's manifesto for the theater, *The Theatre and Its Double* (1938),[1] encompasses several essays, including the producer's conception of the theater of cruelty and the theater of the plague. For Artaud—who is remembered primarily for his dramatic theory rather than his plays—the theater is a liberating force, where repressive social forms are destroyed to reveal the human subconscious in all its desires and instincts. It is a theater which, like the plague, "has been created to drain abscesses collectively,"[2] relieving the audience of the innate cruelty and joy civilization has suppressed. Artaud lamented the death of magic and instinct, and longed for a theater which would duplicate not a quotidian reality but "another archetypal and dangerous reality."[3] Artaud's poetics, as described by Susan Sontag, is "a kind of ultimate, manic Hegelianism in which art is the compendium of consciousness, the reflection of consciousness on itself, and the empty space in which consciousness takes its perilous leap of self-transcendence."[4]

The longings of the theorist are satisfied, at least in part, by the theater of Genet. At the core of Genet's drama is the constant dialectic between illusion and reality, which is dramatically expressed in the relationship between art and the "archetypal reality" of the human subconscious. The characters in Genet's plays are constantly employing art to externalize and give form to their innermost desires. Whether it be the low-life sisters of *The Maids*, the masquerading brothel clientele of *The Balcony*, or the masked Negroes of *The Blacks*, Genet's characters dramatize a vision of illusion as the framework of reality.

In 1920, Jean Genet, then only ten, was arrested for stealing. It was the first of many infractions against society which under French law could have resulted in lifelong incarceration but, because of the efforts of such well-known writers as Claudel, Cocteau, Gide, Mauriac, and Sartre, did not. Some years after the pardon of Genet in 1947, Sartre published a book about the criminal writer, which he entitled *Saint Genet* (1963), embodying the personal paradox of one of France's most controversial literary figures. For Sartre, Genet was the symbol of modern existential man, alienated and in revolt. Genet himself, in his autobiographical *The Thief's Journal*, explains that his revolt took form following a youthful arrest, after which he began to be what society believed him to be, a criminal:

> The mechanism was somewhat as follows (I have used it since): to every charge brought against me, unjust though it be, from the bottom of my heart I shall answer yes. Hardly had I uttered the word—or the phrase signifying it—than I felt within me the need to become what I had been accused of being.[5]

This relationship between the role and the real is at the heart of Genet's drama. Genet's vision of the relationship between the individual and society is one which does not simply acknowledge role playing as an alternate self, whether compatible or incompatible with the real self, but seeks to eliminate the disparity between the two selves through acknowledging their simultaneous existence and absolute interdependence.

It is significant that in each of Genet's plays there is an element of the real in the fictive, of the fictive in the real. In *The Screens*, for example, the playwright specifies that there should be a real object (a wheelbarrow, bucket, bicycle, etc.) next to the screens on which the characters draw the décor. In *The Maids* he suggests juxtaposing realistic props with grotesquely theatrical costumes. In *The Balcony* he dramatizes this contrast by having each brothel patron insist on the presence of an element of the fake in his fantasy. Madame Irma, discussing a potential whorehouse scenario with Carmen, in which her employee will be Saint Theresa, explains, "They all want everything to be as true as possible. . . . Minus something indefinable, so that it won't be true":

> CARMEN: And what'll the authentic detail be?
> IRMA: The ring. He's got it all worked out. The wedding ring. You know that every nun wears a wedding ring, as a bride of God. . . . That's how he'll know he's dealing with a real nun.
> CARMEN: What about the fake detail?
> IRMA: It's almost always the same: black lace under the homespun skirt.[6]

In *The Vision of Jean Genet,* an exceptionally perceptive study of the playwright's life and work, Richard Coe analyzes Genet's theater as a symbol of the dualistic world of reality and illusion. He explains the dualism inherent in art:

> . . . it is precisely at the point where the two meet that poetry is created—the point at which dream is simultaneously reality, where the object is both itself and the revelation of something not-itself. . . .[7]

According to Coe's analysis, the validity of the theater for Genet is to be found in its dependence upon the simultaneous existence of the real and the fictive. In a vacuum of pure illusion, the theater could not exist, for in order for it to be aware of itself as illusion, it must exist in a "context of unrealities."[8] But the reverse side of the coin is also true. Just as illusion can be conceived only in terms of reality, so reality can be conceived only in terms of appearance. The theater, then, itself both real and fake, is a perfect symbol for that duality. And within the theater the metafictional character concentrates that duality even further.

The Maids, the first of Genet's plays to be produced (1947), presents the audience with an ongoing dialectic between reality and illusion on several levels. If Genet's statement in *Our Lady of the Flowers*[9] were adapted to *The Maids,* as Sartre and others have done, adolescent boys rather than women in their thirties, as the text prescribes, would serve as the maids. While director Louis Jouvet cast young girls for the parts in the 1947 Paris production, in 1964 La Mama Experimental Theatre in New York did use adolescent boys. Unfortunately (according to *The Village Voice*), director Tom O'Horgan lacked "a clear directorial viewpoint," making the evening "a camp instead of an illumination."[10] But the production was commendable in its attempt to make explicit the inherent duality of the dramatic character through keeping the audience constantly aware of the simultaneous existence of the real and the fictive. Sartre's introduction to Genet's play (originally the last chapter of *Saint Genet*) expresses a ready understanding of the spirit of Genet's statement. Speaking of the playwright's methods of "de-realization," specifically with respect to the male actors, Sartre notes:

Genet wishes from the very start to strike at the root of the apparent. . . .

　　In order to achieve this absolute state of artifice, the first thing to do is to eliminate nature.[11]

Notwithstanding the fact that an early seventeenth century audience could view a boy Cleopatra without disturbance, simply accepting the theatrical convention, a twentieth-century audience is severely disoriented by the constant presence of the actor, making it exceedingly difficult for it to accept the real persons (the young boys) as the fictive ones (the maids). By refusing to merge the role and the real at this basic level, the playwright creates both a division and a union, for while we are aware of the independent existence of the real and the fictive (the actor and the character), so also are we aware of their simultaneous presence.

　　But even more important than the blatant dichotomy between actor and character is the playwright's complex manipulation of the identities of his central characters, Solange and Claire. The sister maids, in the service of Madame, both love and hate their mistress, one another, and themselves. Frustrated by the constrast between Madame's life of glamor and theirs of kitchen sinks and garrets, the two fill the moments of Madame's absence with a game, which both excites and exhausts them. One pretends to be Madame, the other one of the maids, and they proceed to live out their fantasy by alternating displays of kindness and abuse. The climax of their play is to be the murder of Madame and the supreme glory of the maid who is the murderess.

　　Their role playing, however, is more than a simple case of pretending to be someone one is not. To the extent that the maids play at being characters other than themselves, they have a double dimension much like that created by the feigned madness of Henry IV. When the game-playing identities of the sisters (primarily as Madame and Claire) are juxtaposed with their identities as Claire and Solange as maids, the latter acquire status as their "real" identities, yet when juxtaposed with the blatantly ever-present actor, the identities of Claire and Solange as maids become fictive. The complexity increases when one considers the kinds of roles the maids assume: they are not pretending to be personalities apart from the play world, but assume the identity of another fictive character within Genet's play: Claire becomes Madame, Solange becomes Claire, and, to add to the complexity, in her long speech of imagined glory, Solange is at times herself, at times Claire, and at times Madame.

At no time during their masquerade, however, do we see Claire or Solange solely as the fictive character she is portraying. In addition to the visual division prescribed by Genet, the playwright never allows the acted illusion prolonged sustenance, but repeatedly interrupts it with an intrusion of reality. It is not uncommon for Claire playing Madame, addressing Solange as Claire, to occasionally call her sister Solange, or for Solange playing Claire to refer to herself as Solange or address her masquerading sister as Claire. And at times the game playing is not only interrupted but confused, with one role integrated into another. Note, for example, this early exchange between the sisters:

> SOLANGE: Madame!
> CLAIRE: Am I to be at your mercy for having denounced Monsieur to the police and having sold him? And yet I would have done even worse, or better. You think I haven't suffered? Claire, I forced my hand to pen the letter—without mistakes—the letter that sent my lover to prison.[12]

Although Solange addresses Claire as Madame, Claire responds as herself. She then addresses Solange as Claire, but the content of her sentence indicates she has not ceased viewing herself as Claire (it is Claire who wrote the letter), yet in the same sentence she refers to "my lover," indicating she is also viewing herself as Madame. Each sister, then, is a multiplicity of characters, reflecting the many facets of the self. But Genet's vision goes beyond Pirandello's statement of the relativity of our perception of reality to the equality of reality and illusion. The maids, like the criminal playing the criminal and the actor removed from the character, simultaneously "are-what-they-are and are-what-they-appear." The reality which they create is as real as their reality as maids.

The shifting and symbiotic relationship between reality and

illusion comes together with particular emphasis in two places in the play: the beginning and the end. The opening scene can be experienced with innocence only in production, and then only the first time, for the person who is reading the play (complete with naming of characters) or who is seeing it performed for the second time, knows that the two people he sees initially are not Madame and Claire. Those viewing the play for the first time, however, having willingly suspended their disbelief, are taken in by the illusion, not realizing that Genet's exposition hardly offers the basic conditions of the play's reality. The two characters in fact are Claire and Solange, maids at play while their mistress is not at home. We are therefore oriented into a falsity. With any play we begin by accepting as real what is false, but with *The Maids*, we begin by accepting as real what is false within what is already false. And, of course, if adolescent boys are before us, we are faced with another orientation which prevents us from accepting either falsity as completely real.

Yet Genet does give clues to the falsity of the opening scene: "Madame" (Claire) refers to an affair with Mario, the milkman, an inappropriate remark to be made by Madame; "Madame" (Claire) occasionally calls the maid "Solange" whom she earlier called "Claire," and before the ringing of the alarm which signals the end of the first scene, we see other increasingly extended slips in character, culminating finally in our realization that the two characters we are viewing are not the characters they appear to be, but characters playing characters. (Upon further reflection, of course, we realize the maids are neither Madame nor maids nor even women.) Having been betrayed once, our trust in Genet is never fully restored. But it is precisely this unwillingness to submit totally to the dramatic illusion that Genet is fostering, for drama for Genet "must be so false that it sets our teeth on edge." [13]

The closing scene is similarly an assault on the audience's expectations. By that point Genet's audience is guarded, yet reasonably certain it is capable of sorting out the illusion from the reality. Now the maids, having failed in getting Madame to drink the poisoned tea, are acting out their fantasy once again and are nearing the point of culmination, which time and nerves have allegedly prevented them from reaching previously. Solange imagines the glory, the fame, the admiration that being a murderess would bring, as Claire offers herself as a sacrifice, feeling she will find eternal life in Solange, who will carry on for both of them. Claire (as Madame) drinks the tea intended for Madame and, presumably, dies. But does she? Obviously, Genet is playing on the very nature of drama, which allows resurrected dead actors to bow to the audience's applause, but he is also enshrouding in ambiguity the hold his audience had—or thought it had—on reality. Within the fictive world of the play, is Claire's death "real"? Or is it fictive, simply part of the game the sisters play: has Claire sipped the tea dozens of times before and then risen again to begin a new cycle of the game playing which relieves the tedium of the maids' lives and externalizes their innermost desires? For Genet, either question, despite apparent contradiction, may be answered "yes," because for the sisters there is no preservable distinction between the truth and the lie; for them, fantasy is fulfillment.

A similar kind of merger of reality and illusion is achieved in The Balcony, a play perhaps more confusing in its dramatization of Genet's vision but somewhat less complex in its portrayal of his conception of the self and the role. In The Maids, the frequent transitions of Claire and Solange create a multiplicity of selves, requiring the audience continually to adjust its perception, and finally leaving it holding onto a very slippery dividing line between reality and illusion which it isn't even certain exists. In The Balcony, the real and fictive identities of the brothel clientele are more clearly delineated, and at the end, with the characters' conscious relinquishing of the fiction of their roles and the assumption of the real images of high office, we witness a merger of reality and illusion which leaves us with a curious sense of loss. As in The Maids, the metafictional characters of The Balcony dramatize Genet's continual sense of self and other.

The Balcony has been performed frequently in New York's off-off-Broadway theaters and elsewhere, but with each performance one wonders whether Genet himself would be any more pleased than he was with the first production in London in 1957, which he considered a travesty:

> Instead of giving the play a touch of nobility, it was cheaply vulgarized.
>
> The characters were transformed into grotesque and disgusting puppets, whom even I could not recognize. The director, Peter Zadek, even brought on a pack of whores all got up in lace, who swayed nauseatingly across the stage and whose presence I had never so much as suggested. I intended my characters to be larger than life; they were reduced to caricatures straight out of *Hellzapoppin*.[14]

Yet it is ironic that Genet, who was so exceedingly aware of the significance of external signs in determining reality, and who in fact dramatizes this fact in *The Balcony*, could not anticipate such a production, for surely the setting of a brothel *is* suggestive of "whores all got up in lace." Zadek's response to the text of *The Balcony* is no different from the response of Genet's fellow prisoners the first time he awaited trial: mistakenly attired in a prisoner's uniform rather than in the civilian clothes the as-yet-untried wore, Genet was treated with contempt.[15] Nor is it any different from the response Genet is continually attempting to elicit through the signs of his theater. The Bishop, the Judge, and the General may indeed be "larger than life," but the playwright depends very heavily on external signals to make them so: each of the brothel patrons wears shoulder pads and elevated shoes and the trappings of the profession he is portraying. Zadek's interpretation, then, while perhaps not faithful to Genet's intent, does validate *The Balcony*'s dramatization of the emblematic import of setting and costume, as well as the transforming power of illusion.

Three of Genet's central characters in *The Balcony*, the brothel patrons, function in the first part of the play as both fictive and real characters, assuming, like the maids, metafictional roles from the outset as they play within the play, acting out their scenarios. In place of an uncomplicated submission to the dramatic illusion, the audience, faced with these double characters, is constantly aware of the bifocal vision which, though natural to drama, is not conventionally announced. Impersonating, respectively, a bishop, a judge, and a general, the clients reach orgiastic joy in the Artaudian act of externalizing and hence purging themselves of their deepest, socially repressed desires. As Madame Irma explains: "When it's over, their minds are clear. . . . Suddenly they understand mathematics. They love their children and their country" (p. 35). Yet the very fact of their fiction is essential to these three characters, who, unlike the revolutionaries outside the brothel, are interested only in an imaginative rejection of reality. Each wants only the form of his role, not the function; each wants the illusion and not the reality. Note, for example, the conversation between the Bishop and a brothel employee concerning his granting her absolution for her six deadly sins:

> THE WOMAN: Six, but deadly ones! And it was a job finding those.
> THE BISHOP (uneasy): What? You mean they were false?
> THE WOMAN: They were real, all right!   (p. 9)

Implicit in this conversation is the fact that the man impersonating a bishop knows very well that the sins, as well as the entire scenario, are make-believe, for such is the nature of this "delicious, untroubled state" (pp. 79–80).

In these early scenes, audience and characters alike are very aware of the presence of and the clear division between the two halves of the metafictional character. Yet if Genet creates these opening scenarios to establish the desirability, even the supremacy, of illusion, he both affirms and upsets this judgment in the second part.

The opening scenes of The Balcony have frequently been praised as artistically flawless, the oft-revised closing scenes less so. Kenneth Tynan, for example, reviewing the world première in 1957, wrote:

> The first, or expository, half is flawless; out of an anarchic, unfettered imagination there emerges a perfect nightmare world. But the second half is argumentative, and logic is necessarily a fettered thing, bound by rules to which M. Genet, who has flouted rules all his life, is temperamentally opposed. Just when the play cries out for an incisive, satiric mind like M. Sartre's, it branches off into a confusion so wild that I still cannot understand what the scenes in the rebel camp were meant to convey. As an evoker, M. Genet is magnificent: as an explainer, he is a maddening novice.[16]

A look at the status of the metafictional character, however, shows that in The Balcony Genet has achieved an artistically and philosophically effective merger of reality and illusion.

The focus in the second part of the play moves from the secure studios of the house of illusions to the balcony stretching out above the revolution and symbolizing the buffer zone between the sham and the real. Below the balcony, the revolutionaries are attempting to destroy the palace and houses of government. But though their campaign is founded on reason, the leaders soon find that the rank and file need the unifying force of a symbol for their cause. They designate Chantal, a former employee of Madame Irma's whorehouse, as that symbol: "She doesn't belong to herself any more. She's ours. She's our sign" (p. 56). As Chantal tells Roger: "People say that I soar above the insurrection, that I'm its soul and voice" (p. 55). Recognizing their need for illusion, the Envoy devises a plan whereby the symbols of authority which the revolutionaries thought they had destroyed would appear before the crowds, so the ordinary patrons of the brothel, those who gloried in their impersonations of bishop, judge, and general, don their costumes and step out onto the balcony, just as Chantal falls dead. The plan is successful in quelling the battle; the populace is appeased.

Bishop, Judge, and General, however, are not. In crossing over the boundary separating the fantasy world from the real one to become permanent images of church and state, the brothel patrons have sacrificed their private scenarios for public ones. Now that they are bishop, judge, and general in the eyes of the world, they can no longer step at will in and out of their roles nor enjoy the comfort of knowing their fantasies are fictive, for now they are frozen in their commitment to the form of authority. Recognizing their loss, the Bishop laments:

> So long as we were in a room in a brothel, we belonged to our own fantasies. But once having exposed them, having named them, having proclaimed them, we're now tied up with human beings, tied to you, and forced to go on with this adventure according to the laws of visibility. . . .
>
>   . . . For ours was a happy state. And absolutely safe. In peace, in comfort, behind shutters, behind padded curtains, pro-

tected by a police force that protects brothels, we were able to be a general, judge and bishop to the point of perfection and to the point of rapture! You tore us brutally from that delicious, untroubled state.   (pp. 79–80)

The Judge cries: "I'm just a dignity represented by a skirt" (p. 80). And the General complains:

At no moment can I prepare myself—I used to start a month in advance!—prepare myself for pulling on my general's boots and breeches. I'm rigged in them for all eternity. By Jove, I no longer dream.   (p. 80)

In his preface to The Maids, Sartre describes the circular motion which characterizes Genet's vision of illusion and reality:

He has a vision of an infinitely rapid rotation which merges the poles of appearance and reality, just as, when a multi-colored disk is spun quickly enough, the colors of the rainbow interpenetrate and produce white.[17]

Such a rotation, however, no longer exists for the Bishop, the Judge, and the General; for them, the archetypal reality of their fantasies has prostituted itself to the real world, demolishing their private houses of illusion and removing them permanently from Madame Irma's magic kingdom.

Their metamorphosis is reflected as well in their status as metafictional characters, which by the end of the play ceases to exist. The transformed bishop, judge, and general can no longer stand among the ranks of Genet's dramatis personae who are fictive characters played by fictive characters; they have regressed to the traditional status of their counterparts. Similarly, we as audience can no longer maintain the dialectical balance between the fictive and the real through a constant recognition of the dualism of character. Yet in dramatizing the revolutionaries' need for illusion as well as the brothel patrons' despair over the loss of their fantasy world, Genet has again shown that reality can exist only in a framework of illusion, for, as Tom Driver observes regarding The Balcony, "The 'real' world is saved by the illusory one."[18]

The Balcony appeared in print nearly twenty years after the first production of The Maids (1947). It was around that time that

Genet was asked by an actor to write a play for an all-black cast. But as Genet asks in the introductory note to The Blacks, "what exactly is a black? First of all, what's his color?"[19] Having just a short time earlier turned brothel patrons into high officials of church and state simply through costume, Genet was prepared to respond theatrically to his own questions and dramatize the fact that black is not color but costume and role, not reality but appearance.

The falseness that is present in any definition of "a black" is the same falseness that is present in the theater, where all is simply an image created by playwright and actors. Not content to present his audience with a one-dimensional mirror image of reality, Genet instead exploits the very nature of the theater—its falsity—in order, paradoxically, to recreate reality. For Genet, the more illusion is emphasized, the closer one comes to an understanding of reality, and the more the role is exploited, the closer one comes to understanding the self. The Blacks, therefore, is among the most metatheatrical plays in modern drama.

From the outset, we are not asked to enter the illusion, but are candidly told "it's a performance" (p. 10). We are introduced to the actors as actors, with Archibald explaining that he is a cook, another is a sewing-maid, a third a medical student, and a fourth a curate at St. Anne's (p. 14); throughout the play, whenever there is danger of the intrusion of reality, Archibald or one of the other actors reminds us that "this is the theater" (p. 58), that "it's only play-acting" (p. 87), or that "we are actors and organized an evening's entertainment for you" (p. 99).

More significant than Genet's persistent references to the play as play, however, are the various levels on which the play functions. As with Genet's other dramas, The Blacks is structurally dependent upon (the) play-within-a-play. Just as the maids played at being Madame and the brothel patrons at being high officials, so the characters in The Blacks engage in a play-within-a-play about a ritual killing of a white, a mime show within that ritual, and a backstage play as well in which a Negro traitor is tried and executed. Archibald distinguishes the backstage play from the onstage ritual by cautioning Newport News of the seriousness of the affair: "It's no longer a matter of staging a performance. The man we're holding and for whom we're responsible is a real man" (pp. 81–82). And he distinguishes it from the play itself, which is being viewed by whites:

> As we could not allow the Whites to be present at a deliberation nor show them a drama that does not concern them, and as, in order to cover up, we have had to fabricate the only one that does concern them, we've got to finish this show and get rid of our judges . . . as planned.   (p. 114)

Though kept distinct, each of the plays depends upon the other, and it is in their interplay that they acquire significance as an expression of Genet's philosophy. The play proper, consisting of an all-black cast, is performed for the sake of a white audience. Genet in fact stresses that if at least one white is not present, then a white dummy must be placed in the audience. The ritual rape and murder of a white woman, which contains a mime in which one of the blacks plays the role of the white victim, is performed by blacks for the benefit of whites, who are in reality blacks wearing white masks and sitting on a stage platform. The backstage trial and execution also consists of black performers, but this play is presumably for no audience, for, as we later discover, that action is the "real" action, from which we have been diverted. Genet's technique is to reinforce the white image of blacks, having the actors do what whites would expect of them simply because they are blacks, then to contrast that view of blacks with the backstage action, and in so doing comment on the relationship of the self to the role.

The relationship developed in *The Blacks* is an extension of that suggested by the brothel patrons' permanently becoming bishop, judge, and general, for the blacks in the onstage play perform every action in deference to their social role. The Artaudian freedom of the private, unrepressed self epitomized in *The Balcony*'s opening scenes is Genet's subject only by implication in *The Blacks*, which examines more fully the social self, the role of being what others think we are, or, in Sartrean terms, of becoming the object another's look transfixes us as. For, as Genet shows, though in terms of social reality such a union between self and role may be a valid one, in terms of the more essential, archetypal reality of Artaud, such a union can only be patently false.

One of the Negroes in Genet's play, dressed in ostentatious costume like the others, characterizes a black as an inhuman creature,

> . . . scarred, smelly, thick-lipped, snub-nosed . . . an eater and guzzler of Whites and all other colors, a drooling, sweating, belching, spitting, coughing, farting goat-fucker, a licker of white boots, a good-for-nothing, sick, oozing oil and sweat, limp and submissive.   (p. 27)

This, of course, is the whites' conception of blacks—or, more accurately, the blacks' conception of the whites' conception—and in this play the blacks are set on eliminating any disparity between reality and image. It is the very experience Genet himself had when he found himself labeled thief, homosexual, racketeer, traitor. If this was the image others had of him, then he would validate the picture by playing that role.

But if the onstage play emphasizes this relationship throughout, by its end we discover just how serious Archibald is when he says, "My anger isn't make-believe" (p. 33), and we understand the bitterness and complacency with which he announces, "we are what they want us to be. We shall therefore be it to the very end, absurdly" (p. 126). Dramatizing the whites' image of black is indeed absurd, for there is little basis for that image: there is no black murderer, no white victim, no corpse for the funeral. Indeed, the onstage antics turn out to be the clown show of Genet's subtitle.

Furthermore, if the revelation of the patent falsity of the actions of a play which is already sham is not enough to dispel the stereotype, the report of the backstage action should be, for in that action the trial is carried out in an orderly, civilized fashion, without savagery, with the appropriate persecution and defense arguments, and according to the laws of a respectable—and white—society. The anxiety which the audience experiences when it discovers that the onstage action, especially created for them, has been a diversion from an act which they were not entitled to witness is not fear of revolution, but fear at having witnessed the destruction of the image to which they are committed. For the interplay of reality and illusion among the three or four plays which constitute *The Blacks* firmly attests to the falsity of such an image in both archetypal and social contexts. It is the skillfully realized metatheatrical approach of Genet's play which is responsible for maneuvering the audience into this realization.

Inseparable from the hierarchies of illusion Genet creates in *The Blacks* is the metafictional character. Clearly the people on stage before us are actors, but so also are they fictional characters. But as Ruby Cohn points out, while all the blacks are actors, "different degrees of reality penetrate their roles":

> The dancing Negroes in evening-clothes of "fake elegance" seem more authentic than the Negroes in the Balcony, with garish costumes and white masks, and yet the mock-whites may be more authentic than we, a white audience. Newport News, in his woolen sweater and bare feet, seems more authentic than the Negroes in evening-clothes.[20]

It is precisely this awareness of multiplicity which Genet is committed to preserving which authenticates the reality of the backstage characters. We are not invited into their world of illusion in the traditional sense—indeed, they are not even placed before us on stage—but because we are constantly aware of the dialectic between reality and illusion that is being created on stage, in the contrasting absence of the dialectic backstage, we immediately view the blacks who are part of the trial and execution as real. Though we never witness the backstage action, it is that play which ultimately is *The Blacks*, for it is that play which presents blackness free from the illusion of preconception, apart from the theatrical experience.

The idea of mask and face is made particularly explicit in the characters of the court—queen, missionary, judge, governor, and valet—who are present on stage throughout the play and who function both as audience and participants, as whites and as blacks. Perched upon a balcony, these characters are actually black actors wearing white masks, playing audience to the play of the ritual murder. We are unaware of their blackness until, the backstage action complete, the actors reveal their faces and then, designated by Genet as "the one who played the queen," "the one who played the missionary," etc., they continue without pretension with their obligation to complete the play, descending to the stage to submit themselves for execution. It is these characters who crystallize the dialectic of the play, for with their unmasking, white and black are absorbed into each other, rendering continuation of the play absurd. As masked figures, the characters of the court become metaphors for the dialectic with which Genet is playing; as unmasked white judges—particularly at the point of their murder—they become metaphors for the death of the white image of blackness, which the backstage action secures.

Like the maids, the blacks simultaneously "are-what-they-are" and "are-what-they-appear." For while the play has unequivocally destroyed the image of blackness which whites hold, the reality of this image outside the play remains. For the audience the blacks are at once the vindicated characters before them and the false but stubborn image of blacks which they hold. The power of illlusion to transform reality has been dramatized in what is surely Genet's most patent social lesson: blackness—which is not confined to Negroes, but extends to any outcast group—is as much a pretense, an image, an illusion as it is a reality.

In his preface to The Maids, Sartre recites the example of Epimenides, the Greek philosopher who spoke of the verity of Cretans:

> Epimenides says that Cretans are liars. But he is a Cretan. Therefore he lies. Therefore Cretans are not liars. Therefore, he speaks the truth. Therefore, Cretans are liars. Therefore, he lies, etc.[21]

For Genet, illusion is not only a smokescreen for reality, but also the framework of that reality. Just as the truth of Epimenides leads to the lie, so also does the lie of the theater lead to the truth, "impelling men to see themselves as they are," causing the "mask to fall," revealing "the lie."[22]

In the preface to the 1954 edition of *The Maids*, Genet expressed his artistic goal as

> to do away with characters—which stand up, usually, only by virtue of psychological convention—to the advantage of signs as remote as possible from what they are meant first to signify, though nevertheless attached to them in order, by this sole link, to unite the author with the spectator, in short, so as to contrive that the characters on the stage would be only the metaphors of what they are supposed to represent.[23]

By embodying in his characters the dialectic inherent in the theater and in life and by constantly insisting upon that dialectic, Genet elevates his characters to the status of symbol, a symbol which is perfectly realized in the metafictional character.

৩Three
Beckett's Didi and Gogo, Hamm and Clov

SURELY THE MOST significant dramatic voice of postwar France is that of Samuel Beckett. The Irish-born playwright, a citizen of France since 1938 and a friend of James Joyce, stunned the literary world in 1952 with the production of *Waiting for Godot*, a play which still continues to provoke critical and popular attention. The work of Ionesco, Adamov, Grass, Pinter, Gelber, Stoppard, and dozens of other contemporary playwrights is foreshadowed thematically and formally by Beckett.

The characters of Beckett's plays, from *Waiting for Godot* to those in the dramatic pieces comprising *Ends and Odds*, take their places in a playworld in which the atmosphere is permeated with a sense of the absurd. Invariably, Beckett's characters are metaphors for modern—or universal—man, puzzling over his inability to detect an intelligible pattern and suffering the consequent anguish of a futile search for meaning. The characteristic state of mind of a Beckett character is despair.

But Beckett's portrait of modern man is never detached from the playwright's keen sense of theater. As Katharine Worth points out, Beckett's theater is "intensely physical" drama that is "insistently aware of itself as theatrical process."[1] "Play" for Beckett is conceived in terms of the theater and in terms of a universal human activity which constitutes civilization. It is rendered in an ongoing artistic self-consciousness, through which the playwright achieves a fusion of aesthetics and philosophy, and, finally, offers modern man the illusion of meaning.

By virtue of the self-reflective quality of his theater, virtually every play of Beckett's is populated with metafictional characters. The sole physical presence in *Krapp's Last Tape* (1958), for example, is simultaneously playwright, performer, and audience. The creator of his tapes, Krapp, aging, nearsighted, and hard of hearing, begins to record his last one, his sixty-ninth birthday tape, and nostalgically reacts to his former roles as he listens to the recordings of earlier years. In *Happy Days* (1961), Winnie, buried in sand first up to her waist and then up to her neck, is both actor and audience in a world in which one's actions, limited though they may be, must be witnessed in order to be authenticated; the play ends with Winnie and Willie looking at each other. And, perhaps the most pared-down presentation of self and other, the screenplay *Film* (1964) gives us a clear sense of actor and audience through the unspeaking characters of O and E, observed and observer, who in the end merge into one man's self-perception.

Among the more extended examples of Beckett's sense of the theatricality of life is *Waiting for Godot*, in which Didi and Gogo, surely the playwright's best-known dramatic creations, function as metafictional characters. As one of Beckett's several dramatic pairs, the tramps have been credited with both psychological and philosophical duality. G. C. Barnard, for example, calls them a "pseudocouple" who represent "two halves of one human mind . . . indissolubly bound," Vladimir the emotional and practical side and Estragon the withdrawn self.[2] Eugene Webb sees them as a "composite Everyman," embodying "complementary aspects of human nature: Vladimir the intellectual side of man, Estragon the corporeal."[3] More important for our purposes, however (and probably for Beckett's), is the fact of the tramps' "twofoldness" in theatrical terms. As John Fletcher and John Spurling note in *Beckett: A Study of His Plays*: ". . . the sense of being in a theatre, qua theatre, is certainly something the play [*Godot*] relies upon implicitly."[4] Like those of Pirandello and Genet before them, Beckett's characters are double characters as the direct result of the playwright's self-consciousness. Supremely aware of his characters not only as characters but as participants in theater, Beckett endows his tramps with a duality of which the audience is constantly aware. In Didi and Gogo, Beckett purposely and purposefully emphasizes the inherent duality of the dramatic character, so that our vision of them is always double. The tramps are for us, simultaneously, participants in "life" (the playworld) and participants in theater; they are, noticeably and unforgettably, both characters and actors.

Beckett, however, does not achieve this twofoldness by creating an alternate reality for his characters (as Pirandello does in *Henry IV* through the protagonist's madness or Genet does in *The Maids* through the sisters' fantasies). Beckett's characters need not take on another identity, shift back and forth between roles, or even break the dramatic illusion in order to be metafictional characters. Rather, they acquire their duality through the use of language which must be constantly interpreted on two levels. When considered in their other dimension, remarks which constitute the philosophical construct of the play become remarks which serve to self-dramatize the tramps as well.

A selection of the double-edged comments made by Didi and Gogo will illustrate the way in which their remarks function in both philosophical and aesthetic terms, demanding that the audience respond simultaneously on both levels.

Early in the first act of *Waiting for Godot*, Vladimir commands Estragon to "show," but Estragon replies, "There's nothing to show."[5] Didi and Gogo are participants in theater, but have the unique problem of having nothing to show. Significantly, they are successful in showing "nothing," both philosophically and formally, in the first case by showing an existence composed of a spiritual and active void, and in the second, by disregarding the traditional concept of theater that includes dramatic action. In Didi and Gogo's world, there is, indeed, "nothing to be done" (p. 7).

Also early in the play, Vladimir welcomes Estragon back: "So there you are again" and "I'm glad to see you back" (p. 7).

Together after having been apart for the night, they are ready to celebrate their reunion. The characters, of course, have spent the night sleeping (Gogo in a ditch) and have returned to each other in the morning. But the reunion also has significance for the other portion of Didi and Gogo's identities: as actors, they have been apart after the prior day's performance of the play and have once more returned, aware that they will have to come back again the next day.

Several times during the course of the play Didi and Gogo try to leave, but must remind themselves they cannot, for they are waiting for Godot. Their confinement is not only a restriction to that spot along the roadside, beneath the tree, where they are justifying their existence by waiting; it is also a confinement to the stage itself, necessitated by the boundaries of space and time imposed upon them by the very fact that they are actors and must fulfill their commitment to the audience.

The supreme awareness Didi and Gogo have of themselves (or, rather, their creator has of them) as participants in theater is apparent in their various dramatizations of the processes of theater. Their running commentary on the progress of the play reflects their awareness of the presence of an audience. Some of their comments reflect their consciousness of themselves in relation to that audience: upon Pozzo's and Lucky's second entrance, for example, Vladimir assures anyone who feels the play is dragging, "We were beginning to weaken. Now we're sure to see the evening out" (p. 49). And as we approach the end of the play, we are again comforted by Vladimir, who assures us, "It is very near the end of its repertory" (p. 55). Other comments reveal that the tramps at moments actually become the audience: Vladimir remarks, "Charming evening we are having" (p. 23), and, later, "This is awful!" (p. 41), "This is becoming really significant" (p. 44), and "I've been better entertained" (p. 26). And Estragon says, "I find this really most extraordinarily interesting" (p. 9). Vladimir even asks Estragon to save his seat when he must interrupt their conversation to urinate. Insofar as Didi and Gogo are commenting on the emptiness of their existence and on the nearly unendurable task of waiting for Godot, each of these comments has a serious place within the philosophical construct of the play. But when viewed as comments made by the other portion of the double character, that portion which reflects Beckett's awareness of his art, the comments are funny, for they force the audience into experiencing a phenomenon not expected in theater: seeing itself as audience.

While conveying a comic sense of both the theatrical event and man's condition in life is surely part of Beckett's purpose in creating the tramps' duality, it is his vision of the dramatic quality of life which emerges as the significant reason for the double characters' existence. In responding to Pozzo's cry for help, Vladimir points to a fundamental tenet of the dramatic experience:

> But at this place, at this moment of time, all mankind is us, whether we like it or not. . . . Let us represent worthily for once the foul brood to which a cruel fate consigned us!   (p. 51)

As characters in Beckett's play, Didi and Gogo are universal man (they are "Cain and Abel," "Adam," "all humanity"), but so also are they universal man as actors. Through the sustained double identification of the tramps as both characters and actors, Beckett creates a metaphor not just for universal man but for universal man *as actor.*

Yet in remaining actors, the characters in the play are never totally integrated with the world of the play. Their self-conscious remarks repeatedly remind us of their presence as actors. They are constantly drawing attention to what Robbe-Grillet calls the "essential thing about a character in a play": the fact that he is *there.*[6] As Enoch Brater has pointed out, the awareness of "presence" is characteristic as well of Camus' philosophy of absurd man, who "takes his daily reality as nothing more than a stage set."[7] What is important in Camus, however, as in the theater of Beckett, is that neither man nor the universe creates the absurdity, but rather the disjunction between them does. In *Godot* the constant reminders that Didi and Gogo are not simply characters but participants in a dramatic event creates a division between the characters and their world which becomes a metaphor for absurd man, unable to reconcile his self to his universe.

The world of Didi and Gogo is a patternless one, with salvation meted out on an arbitrary basis by a god that may not even exist. It is characterized by Lucky's speech, which defines civilization as "shards of religion, philosophy, science, art, sport, and modern industry."[8] The only god in such a world is one whose love admits exceptions: the gospel of Luke tells the story of the two thieves crucified with Christ, one of whom was saved, the other damned; the boy who tends the goats for Godot is treated kindly by his master, while the boy who tends the sheep is beaten; Pozzo and Lucky are in reasonably good health in the first act, but in the second, Pozzo is blind and Lucky dumb. For Didi and Gogo, the chance of salvation is, at best, fifty-fifty. And the choice of salvation is arbitrary: "Given the existence . . . of a . . . god . . . with white beard . . . who . . . loves us dearly with some exceptions for reasons unknown but time will tell . . . man wastes and pines" (pp. 28–29).

Yet Didi and Gogo are actors, and as such not only remind us of the rift between man and his universe but also of the responsibility of universal man to act. In response to Pozzo's call for help, Vladimir urges Estragon:

> Let us not waste our time in idle discourse! (Pause. Vehemently.) Let us do something, while we have the chance! It is not every day that we are needed. Not indeed that we personally are needed. Others would meet the case equally well, if not better. . . . Let us make the most of it, before it is too late!   (p. 51)

The responsibility, the dilemma, the desperation expressed by Vladimir are shared by universal man, who, like the tramps, is trying to show what this "fact of being there consists in."[9] But, like Didi and Gogo, man cannot progress beyond the recognition of this responsibility; all his activities can only result in the illusion of meaning.

The constant activity of Didi and Gogo is game play. One game involves a routine of silent action in which Vladimir's and Lucky's hats are manipulated from one hand to another; another involves exercises in which the tramps in turn hop from one foot to the next. Most of their games, however, are verbal ones, carefully constructed. They decide to "make a little conversation" and begin by contradicting one another:

ESTRAGON: Let's contradict each other.
VLADIMIR: Impossible.   (p. 41)

They ask each other questions:

ESTRAGON: Que voulez-vous?
VLADIMIR: I beg your pardon?   (p. 42)

They abuse each other:

VLADIMIR: Moron!
ESTRAGON: Vermin!
VLADIMIR: Abortion!
ESTRAGON: Curate!
VLADIMIR: Cretin!
ESTRAGON (with finality): Critic!   (p. 48)

And they play at making up:

VLADIMIR: Gogo!
ESTRAGON: Didi!
VLADIMIR: Your hand!
ESTRAGON: Take it!
VLADIMIR: Come to my arms!   (p. 48)

At the end of one of their linguistic games the tramps congratulate themselves. Estragon boasts: "That wasn't such a bad little canter" (p. 42). And at the end of another, Vladimir notes, "How time flies when one has fun!" (p. 49).

Earlier the tramps had attempted storytelling but were unsuccessful. When Vladimir told the story of the four gospels and the crucifixion of Christ and the two thieves, he had to plead with the unresponsive Estragon to respond: "Come on, Gogo, return the ball, can't you, once in a way?" (p. 9). When Estragon told the story of the Englishman in the brothel, Vladimir screamed at him to stop. The storytelling forced one of the actors into an unnatural and independent role, which the two, being actors, could not accept. The games, however, are successful because each involves the full participation of both tramps as actors.

Each of their games, however, is short-lived: there are a few lines of dialogue, the game is complete, and then there is silence. Between games Didi and Gogo feel the same desperation as that of the woman in T. S. Eliot's "A Game of Chess" in The Waste Land, who cries, "What shall I do now? What shall I do? . . . What shall we do to-morrow? What shall we ever do?" While the completion of each game brings self-congratulation, it also brings the awareness that they must find something to do next. Both philosophically and theatrically, the tramps must play, and as actors they are constantly aware that the completion of each acting game (or each scene) brings with it the obligation to play another.

The greatest game the tramps play is waiting. It is certainly true, both theatrically and metaphysically, that "nothing happens," "nobody comes," and "there's nothing to be done." There is no plot progression in Godot, no causal relationship between events, no linear sequence. Time is a confused, timeless "now." The play does not say how many times Didi and Gogo have met to wait, nor do the tramps themselves know. Have they been together for "a million years" (p. 7), or "fifty years" (p. 35), or only since yesterday? Didi and Gogo try to remember the details of a past life in the Mâcon country, but cannot, and they are not even certain that they were there. Similarly, they are not sure whether the messenger from Godot is appearing or reappearing, or even that he is the same boy. When they try to reconstruct the activities of the preceding day, they cannot even confirm that it was yesterday that they met Pozzo and Lucky. With Pozzo, they can only conclude that everything happens or happened "one day" (p. 57); they cannot say which day.

And we ourselves cannot verify anything. The stage directions tell us Act II takes place "Next day. Same time. Same place." But the bare tree has sprouted leaves, and Pozzo and Lucky have gone blind and dumb. According to our logical scheme of time, such drastic changes could not have taken place overnight, and we cannot trust our own conceptions of logical, sequential time. Like Pozzo, we have lost our watches, and with Vladimir we can say, "Time has stopped" (p. 24). Life in the world of Didi and Gogo is a piling up and repetition of moments, none of which bears any causal relationship to another, none of which is meaningful, but all of which constitute the waiting. And it is the waiting to which Didi and Gogo are committed. Despite the fact that Godot does not come, they insist upon waiting, until the waiting itself becomes an activity which seems to give meaning and pattern to their lives. Estragon says to Vladimir: "We don't manage too badly, eh Didi, between the two of us? We always find something, eh Didi, to give us the impression that we exist" (p. 44). The tramps are aware that it is only through action that they—or universal man—can confront the universe, yet all they can offer is activity.

There is one game, however, that Didi and Gogo consider but reject (despite the attractiveness of its side effects), and that is hanging themselves. They do not have the means of hanging both, and they will not consider hanging just one. Despite their own repeated suggestions that each would be better off alone, Didi and Gogo will not separate. Vladimir reminds Estragon: ". . . but for me . . . where would you be. . . . You'd be nothing more than a little heap of bones at the present minute . . ." (p. 7). Their need for one another is the universal need of isolated man for fellow human beings. Even more importantly, in rejecting hanging, the tramps are rejecting what may be the only meaningful choice available to them, the one choice which would turn their activity into action. Instead they choose to continue their frivolous play and futile wait. With levity, they claim they are waiting for Godot because they are curious to see what he looks like, but the truth of their commitment is much deeper: waiting has been their entire existence, and they cannot acknowledge that it is worthless.

But there is another reason why the tramps cannot go through with the hanging: quite simply, it would end their play. As actors, Didi and Gogo are confined to the stage, jointly committed to repeat game after game, night after night. Their bonds are as real as the rope that ties Lucky to Pozzo, and the tramps know this. When Pozzo has a difficult time leaving after bidding the tramps adieu, he remarks, "I don't seem to be able to depart" (p. 31). At the end of each of the two acts, Didi and Gogo resolve to go, yet they do not:

> ESTRAGON: Well, shall we go?
> VLADIMIR: Yes, let's go.
>
> *They do not move.*   (p. 35)

They must continue to play, but the one game they cannot play is ending their play. Such a game would violate their commitment, burst open the boundaries, and destroy the game. Repeatedly they return to contemplate suicide, but they never consummate that game.

The pathetic heroes of *Waiting for Godot* may understand that man's alternative to absurdity is action, but they are themselves unable to act. Game play and waiting, activity and nonaction, are the best they offer, and the illusion of meaning is the most they achieve. It is worth noting the continuation of Lucky's speech: ". . . man . . . wastes and pines . . . in spite of the strides of physical culture the practice of sports such as tennis football running cycling swimming flying floating riding gliding conating camogie skating tennis of all kinds dying flying sports . . . of all kinds. . . ." (p. 29). The catalogue is, of course, unimportant; what is important is the recognition that man spends his life playing games, games of all kinds, not merely of organized sport, but of life: games of language and activity, the same kinds of games Didi and Gogo play. Nevertheless, man wastes and pines. Games can pass the time, they can constitute existence, but they can give life only the illusion of meaning, for, like Beckett's play, they do not constitute (an) action.

Vladimir expresses this awareness once. Following his moment of reflection on the philosophical nature of life ("Astride of a grave . . . the gravedigger puts on the forceps" [p. 58]), the messenger boy conveys a crucial bit of information to him: Godot has a white beard. On hearing the news, Vladimir cries out, "Christ have mercy on us!" (p. 59). He obviously recalls that Lucky's god, the gratuitous god to whom salvation is a fifty-fifty proposition, has a white beard too. After a moment of violent emotion in which Vladimir lunges at the boy, Vladimir rejoins Estragon to tell him they cannot leave, for they must wait for Godot. Every prior reminder which Vladimir had given Estragon was, "We are waiting for Godot." Now he says resolutely, "We *have* to come back to-morrow. To wait for Godot" (p. 59, emphasis mine). Vladimir knows that the only meaning they have is in the waiting, for there can be no fulfillment. But he can only reject his epiphany, for acceptance would be as final and destructive as the hanging game they could not play. So he resumes the game. Godot is a disillusionment; their waiting has no potential, but so long as they have the waiting, they have the *illusion* of meaning, which Vladimir prefers to absurdity. Act II ends as did Act I:

> VLADIMIR: Well? Shall we go?
> ESTRAGON: Yes, let's go.
>
> *They do not move.*   (p. 60)

Vladimir and Estragon have meaning only in the world of (the) play, a world in which illusion is of the essence.

In realistic drama we are aware that playing is an imitation of living. In *Waiting for Godot* we are aware that playing is living or, to reverse the statement, that living is playing, and, consequently, all that is left to modern man is illusion. Didi and Gogo's significance as a philosophical metaphor is extended from universal man hopelessly waiting to universal man needfully playing. And as such, Beckett's self-reflectiveness is inseparable from his philosophical vision, which is that in the absence of meaning, it is only in play and art that universal man can find justification for his existence, for play and art offer him the illusion of meaning.

Endgame (1957), performed four years after the first production of *Godot,* is similarly informed with the sense of the highly theatrical quality of life which was to characterize all of Beckett's plays. The title itself, *Fin de partie* in French, refers to the final phase of a chess game, and Beckett, writing of the 1967 Berlin production, said: "*Endgame* is only play. Nothing less."[10] In terms of their self-consciousness, *Endgame* and *Godot* are in many respects complementary.

Like their predecessors the tramps, Hamm and Clov, the couple in Endgame, comment throughout on the progress of the play. Any of their wry remarks—"This is slow work," [11] "This is not much fun" (p. 13), "This is deadly" (p. 28), "Things are livening up" (p. 29), "We're getting on" (p. 68)—may be attributed to the tramps just as readily as to the strange couple who occupy the dreary room of Endgame. Hamm and Clov know very well that they are actors in a play. Hamm, in fact, has "All kinds of fantasies! That I'm being watched" (p. 70). And, in the same kind of acknowledgment of audience expressed by Didi and Gogo when they looked out over the stage and joked about the bog out there, Clov peers through his telescope and reports, "I see . . . a multitude . . . in transports . . . of joy" (p. 29).

Like the tramps, Hamm and Clov are confined to a given area, but in their case, the restriction is a far more rigid one. Didi and Gogo could neither hang themselves nor leave; they had to keep returning to the tree to wait for Godot, and to fulfill their obligations as actors. But they were able to extend their space to the backstage area. As Katharine Worth [12] has so ably shown, the backstage world is very much a part of Didi and Gogo's world, and we are constantly reminded of its presence through the frequent exits and entrances of the tramps, Pozzo and Lucky, and the boy. The backstage world is the imaginary world to which the tramps retreat to sleep, the Mâcon country where they once worked, and the place from which Godot will surely come. But it is also a real backstage, with a men's room at the "end of the corridor, on the left" (p. 23).

The characters of Endgame inhabit a far more claustrophobic and containing world. They are in a boxlike room with undersized windows which one can reach only by ladder, and a door so small Beckett calls it an "aperture." Hamm is not only blind, but confined to a wheelchair, and Nagg and Nell live out the remnants of their existences in trash cans. The images of isolation enforce the philosophic vision of this postcataclysmic world, but so also do they underscore the fact that the characters before us are actors, limited to the stage and obligated to stay. While Hamm can turn circles in his wheelchair, only Clov is truly mobile. As if affirming this mobility, he frequently walks backstage to the kitchen, where he stands staring at the wall. But this backstage area is every bit as confining as the room itself; more significant is the greater backstage area, the world which Clov views through the windows and into which he does not venture until, possibly, the end of the play. Clov's inability to leave entirely is not simply because he is not emotionally ready for it, but, as his final gesture of possible departure shows, his leaving would end the play. As he prepares to don his tweed coat and panama hat, Clov remarks, "This is what we call making an exit" (p. 81). Hamm too conceives Clov's departure—if indeed Clov does depart—in terms of play. Calling to his charge and receiving no answer, he resolves, "Since that's the way we're playing it . . . let's play it that way . . . and speak no more about it . . . speak no more" (p. 84). Indeed, without dialogue, there is nothing left for Hamm, the eternal actor suggested by his name, but his final soliloquy.

While many of the same observations concerning Beckett's vision of man may be made about *Endgame* and *Godot*, the later play is clearly a refinement and further development in terms of theatrical technique. The self-consciousness of Didi and Gogo, while effective in delineating the relationship of self to role, of reality to illusion, only suggests the perfectly realized metafictional characters of *Endgame*. For as Ross Chambers observes in "An Approach to *Endgame*," Hamm as actor first " 'represents' what he cannot 'be'," but ultimately "represents *instead* of being." [13]

Actually, it is Hamm who is at the center of the action, a fact which Beckett alludes to by Hamm's insistence that Clov wheel him along the perimeter of the room and then place him exactly in the center. Hamm's first words, repeated twice in the play, are "Me to play," which are followed by the blind man's measured gesture of wiping his glasses and then the inflated classical rhetoric, "Can there be misery—(he yawns)—loftier than mine?" Hamm, though, is more than actor. Like Pozzo, he is playwright and director as well. He creates the chronicle of his past life, writes scenarios about Clov's leaving, and dominates the others with his cruelty. The stage is Hamm's house, Hamm's kingdom, and Hamm controls its occupants. "There's one thing I'll never understand," says Clov. "Why I always obey you. Can you explain that to me?" (p. 77), and when Clov implores Hamm, "Let's stop playing!" Hamm authoritatively replies, "Never" (p. 77). But as Antony Easthope points out in "Hamm, Clov, and Dramatic Method in *Endgame*," Hamm's dominance and cruelty are rendered suspect by his language, which points to an artistic rather than a psychological motivation:

> It is this continuous self-consciousness in Hamm's words and tone of voice which inhibit us from ascribing his cruelty to an impulse beyond the need for rhetorical coherence in the role he plays.[14]

Language in *Endgame* is even more intensely theatrical than in *Godot*, for in *Endgame* virtually every line which is spoken is part of the performance which Hamm directs. The yawn which punctuates Hamm's misery plaint intrudes to remind us that Hamm's suffering is his act, just as every display of pain or emotion is rendered inauthentic by the words which follow. He screams, "What'll I do?" then turns calmly to Clov, who is removing the picture from the wall, and asks "What are you doing?" (p. 72). Infuriated at Nell, he orders Clov to screw down the lid of her trash can, but then unemotionally remarks, "My anger subsides, I'd like to pee" (p. 24). Hamm asks Clov whether he loves him, then engages in this exchange:

> HAMM: I've made you suffer too much. (*Pause.*) Haven't I?
> CLOV: It's not that.
> HAMM (*shocked*): I haven't made you suffer too much?
> CLOV: Yes!
> HAMM (*relieved*): Ah you gave me a fright.
>
> (pp. 6–7)

Hamm, as director and actor, fears the performance is not adequate.

Similarly, a closer look at the rhetoric reveals a curious combination of the classical set speech reminiscent of Kyd's *The Spanish Tragedy* or Shakespeare's *Richard III* and music-hall repertoire. Their dialogue regarding the telescope might serve as example:

HAMM: Look at the earth.
CLOV: I've looked.
HAMM: With the glass?
CLOV: No need of the glass.
HAMM: Look at it with the glass.
CLOV: I'll go and get the glass. (*Exit Clov.*)
HAMM: No need of the glass! (*Enter Clov with telescope.*)
CLOV: I'm back again, with the glass.

(p. 28)

Or:

CLOV: So you all want me to leave you.
HAMM: Naturally.
CLOV: Then I'll leave you.
HAMM: You can't leave us.
CLOV: Then I won't leave you. (*Pause.*)
HAMM: Why don't you finish us? (*Pause.*) I'll tell you the combination of the cupboard if you promise to finish me.
CLOV: I couldn't finish you.
HAMM: Then you won't finish me. (*Pause.*)
CLOV: I'll leave you, I have things to do.

(p. 37)

Clearly Hamm and Clov have recited their lines many times before. Clov complains, "All life long the same questions, the same answers" (p. 5), and later asks, "Why this farce, day after day?" (p. 32). The answer is that this farce or play, this dialogue, is the only existence they have. When Clov demands to know, "What is there to keep me here?" Hamm replies, "The dialogue" (p. 58). For the inhabitants of the shelter the distinction between character and actor has ceased to exist.

Hamm's chronicle, though clearly a fictional account and as such a theatrical event within the play, is *Endgame*'s only offering of psychological realism, the only means through which we get to know the character, rather than the actor, Hamm. The real subject of Hamm's story is not the cruel master who refuses the child food, but Hamm's own life, and particularly his relationship with Clov. And here, rather than consciously enacted suffering, Hamm seems to experience genuine misery, even the need for Clov's forgiveness. As Antony Easthope has suggested, Hamm appears to be obsessed with the need to tell his tale, and he shows genuine signs of disturbance following the telling, including a prayer to God and a plea to Clov to kiss him.[15] Ironically—though it is surely precisely how a play-within-a-play works—the inner action, the experience of Hamm's chronicle, reflects on the outer action, in this case justifying the patently false outer action, the dialogue of suffering, which now becomes more than just acting for its own sake, but a comment on, and an imitation of, reality.

Perhaps the difference in the metafictional characters of *Endgame* and *Godot* is ultimately only a matter of degree. In *Godot* we are reminded frequently of the dialectic between the character and the actor, the self and the role. This is in large part the result of the fact that the world of waiting under the tree achieves dramatic status as the real world, into which Didi and Gogo as actors can never be fully integrated. In *Endgame*, the world of the shelter is created completely by play. In fact, were it not for Hamm's chronicle, we could say of *Endgame*, self *is* role, nothing more, and that all is play, nothing less. Surely Beckett attributes validity to the play quality of life, yet even in *Endgame* he never completely denies the existence of an essential self. The figure of Clov poised for his exit offers a possible, tentative, tenuous hope, which, though not much, does redeem the gloom of the world of Hamm's kingdom. Similarly, Hamm's chronicle, though only obliquely genuine, tentatively affirms the reality of self.

Hamm and Clov, as survivors of a holocaust, are continuing the old way of life, which sustained itself on the illusion of meaning. Now Clov has the chance to try something different, to live in the other world, the backstage world, where games do not exist. With respect to that world Beckett teasingly juxtaposes images of barrenness with images of rejuvenation, remaining noncommittal as to the probable success of Clov's venture. It may well be that Clov, like Didi and Gogo, will discover the necessity of illusion and return to Hamm or create his own games instead; all we have even to suggest the hope of a better life for Clov "out there" is the playwright's indirect suggestion that for Hamm, and hence for all of us, there is an essential self.

Hamm and Clov, then, like Didi and Gogo and so many of

Beckett's other creations, are double characters, with identities that exist beyond those of the traditional fictive character. Perhaps more effectively than any modern playwright, Beckett's metafictional characters serve as metaphors for the relationship of life and art, reality and illusion, the self and the role.

&Four

Weiss's Inmates at Charenton

IN 1964, PETER WEISS's *The Persecution and Assassination of Jean-Paul Marat as Performed by the Inmates of the Asylum of Charenton Under the Direction of the Marquis de Sade* premièred in West Berlin. A year later it was staged in London and New York under the direction of Peter Brook, who also did a film version in 1967. Though Weiss has been relatively productive as a writer of both prose works and plays, it is *Marat/Sade* which is responsible for securely establishing his international reputation.

While *Marat/Sade* creates its own unique dramatic world, it is, perhaps more than any other play in modern drama, an eclectic piece of work, its most apparent literary influences being Beckett, Artaud, Genet, Pirandello, and Brecht. The underlying sense of absurdity which characterizes Beckett's plays is very much a part of Weiss's work as well, which may be as much the result of a literary affinity as it is of Weiss's past, for the young Weiss was among those self-exiled German Jews who managed to leave Germany before World War II. Indeed, as a Swedish citizen (or, as he calls himself, a citizen of the world), Weiss was also to experience a sense of alienation and guilt for which he felt the need for literary expression. His concern with art as a form of purification suggests Artaud. His concern with the significance of role (should he as a Jew have gone to the concentration camp with the others?) suggests Genet; so does his dramatic technique of a play-within-a-play-within-a-play, as in Genet's *The Blacks*. His dramatization of the fluid nature of reality is reminiscent of Pirandello, and his emphasis on the social role (presented in an episodic framework) is very like Brecht, who, like Weiss, admittedly used the theater as a political forum.

More than any of his literary influences, though, Weiss created a drama which, like Wagnerian opera, may be called a *Gesamtkunstwerk*, a total work of art. As Carl Enderstein argues in "The Symbiosis of the Arts and Peter Weiss's *Marat/Sade*,"

> In the kaleidoscopic form of this drama, Weiss has found for the first time the extraordinary vehicle to unleash his many talents simultaneously, incorporating not only various characteristics of different literary genres in his work, but actually creating a *Gesamtkunstwerk* of a sort, by utilizing word, picture and tone (sound.) [1]

Within that kaleidoscope there is not only a fusion of the arts, but also a constantly changing perspective on both the individual and history, through which Weiss presents questions *Marat/Sade* does not attempt to resolve.

One of these questions is that of extreme individuality as opposed to social commitment, ideals which are represented on the one hand by the Marquis de Sade and on the other by Jean-Paul Marat. Sade, perched atop a stool from which he directs the play he wrote, engages in a debate with Marat, surrounded by the soothing waters of his bath, and both present arguments that are convincing and sound. The dialectic is one experienced by Weiss himself in the early 1960s, when he had not yet made the political commitment he felt so necessary for a sense of one's self, and though just a year after *Marat/Sade* he was to decide on Marxism and claim he had intended Marat's side of the argument to prevail, the dialectic remains both dramatically and rationally unresolved.

For our purposes, though, the political milieu of the play is not its most significant feature. This brilliantly conceived metadrama is a series of reflecting surfaces that offer us a perpetually shifting view of self, reality (as history), and art. The asylum at Charenton is a natural breeding ground for metafictional characters.

In 1808 in France, which is the time—or one of the times—and place—or one of the places—during which *Marat/Sade* operates, it was quite usual for the aristocratic Parisian population to visit insane asylums for an afternoon's entertainment. And, as if the antics of the madmen were not enough to satisfy this curious (though readily documentable in other countries and times as well) taste, the inmates would stage an organized performance for their audience. It is one such performance which becomes the play-within-a-play of Weiss's *Marat/Sade* and which is responsible for creating the beginnings of multiplicity for Weiss's metafictional characters.

As in Genet's *The Blacks*, when the *dramatis personae* are presented, they are designated both by their "reality" and their role. All but Coulmier are inmates of the clinic who, for purposes of rehabilitation through art, are acting out roles in a kind of psychodrama depicting the assassination of Jean-Paul Marat. A paranoid plays the role of Marat, a sexual deviant the role of Jacques Roux, the revolutionary priest, and a young woman who suffers from sleeping sickness the role of Charlotte Corday, who stabbed Marat in his bath. A group of four inmates functions as chorus, commenting on the action and creating through song and mime the play's emotional effect. And Sade, the author of the play but himself an inmate, directs.

So that there be no forgetting that the production is a stage show, the director of the clinic, M. Coulmier, is everpresent, offering a prologue and an epilogue, interrupting whenever he is disturbed by the argument or the inmates' reactions, and sitting with his family on an elevated platform, reminding us that they are an audience within the larger audience (the Parisian elite) within yet a larger audience (ourselves). Weiss could not announce more clearly that this is a play. Yet there is an element of reality involved as well. Historically Corday did indeed kill Marat, and the inmates' play will be a reenactment of an historical event.

The device of madmen playing historical figures is especially effective when we consider Weiss's characters in their metafictional status. The duality of the *dramatis personae*, of which
an audience responding to the metafictional character is ever
aware, is indeed present here, but in this case that duality
requires a complicating qualification. The character (whom we
would normally view as the fictive self) is in this case an historical figure, hence every bit as real as the actor himself. On the
other hand, the actor (whom we normally view as the real self) is
in this case one who lives in a world of illusions, a framework of
unreality which characterizes his madness. And if the duality
functions, as it normally does, to remind us of the inherent duality implicit in *any* dramatic character, we are one dimension
further removed, and every part of the show, even the reality of
the inmates, becomes sham.

What Weiss is asking is, "How accurate is our conception
not only of Marat's murder, but of history at all?" Already com-
bining and confusing illusion and reality by virtue of its being
simultaneously stage and history, the event takes on additional
perspective by the fact that it is fictionalized in 1808, fifteen
years later than its historical occurrence. The time gap is obliquely but certainly a reference to the contemporary German situation which, as Sidney F. Parham has noted, would surely be
noticed by Weiss's 1964 audience:

> There are fifteen years between the murder of Marat and the pre-
> sentation of Sade's play. The same number of years separate the
> audience from the founding of the Bundesrepublik.[2]

It is this audience which must judge the certainty of Coulmier's
parting remarks, which insist upon 1808 France—and 1964 Germany—as an enlightened age:

> For today we live in far different times. We have no oppressors, no
> violent crimes and although we're at war anyone can see it can
> only end in victory.[3]

Surely by the epilogue the audience, having been led through
the maze of mirrors reflecting within mirrors until they become
fun house distortions, recognizes the gravity with which Weiss

is commenting on the inability of man to know, much less to understand, his past.

Equally important is Weiss's question regarding the self. The extreme individuality for which Sade argues is quite alien to the collectivism of Weiss's chosen Marxist philosophy, yet when one turns to the author's autobiographical works, one can clearly see the affinity Weiss had for Sade's search for self. Arguing against revolution, Sade, in his dialogue with Marat, states:

> Before deciding what is wrong and what is right
> first we must find out what we are
> I
> do not know myself
> No sooner have I discovered something
> than I begin to doubt it
> and I have to destroy it again
> What we do is just a shadow of what we want to do
> and the only truths we can point to
> are the ever-changing truths of our own experience   (p. 31)

A passage in Weiss's *Vanishing Point* (1962) points to a similar quest on the part of the author:

> I stepped out into the stream of human beings, went along the Boulevard [in Paris], among young, open faces, among laughing eyes, among the tall, proud figures of Africans, went through the parks, in museums and libraries, sat on the terraces of cafés, and instead of winning something of this new life for myself, hour by hour I lost more of myself, until my own name became uncertain to me. . . .[4]

Describing the moment experienced when he discovered his language, Weiss continues:

> Now I could show who I was, what kind of I it had been that I had carried through the years of exile, that I had saved from being annihilated on the battlefield and in the gas chamber. . . . This freedom was absolute, I could lose myself in it, and I could find myself in it again; I was able to abandon all, all striving, all belonging, and I could start to speak again.[5]

Yet the certainty of the discovery of self which the passage from *Vanishing Point* reflects is undercut by Weiss's experimental novels. As Hans-Bernhard Moeller points out:

> While integrity and integration of the individual predominates in
> the preceding creations [Leavetaking (1961) and Vanishing Point]
> the unifying structure of a protagonist's personality is abolished in
> the two experimental novels, The Shadow of the Coachman's
> Body [1960] and The Conversation of the Three Walking Men
> [1963]. Both recall Weiss's own description of Strindberg's con-
> cept of man: a collage in flux rather than a unified character.[6]

And it is further undercut by the multiplicity of selves to be
found in the two characters who engage in the Marat-Sade debate. Marat achieves his multiplicity through our awareness that
it is a paranoid who is playing his role; through the presence of
his alter-ego, Roux; and through the appearance of visions[7] of
his former self, seen through the eyes of schoolmaster, parents,
and others. These combine to question the purity of Marat's de-
dication to the cause of revolution, pointing to a personal and
persistent psychological motive and suggesting that Marat's
commitment may not be to the populace, but to the self. Sade, on
the other hand, plays only himself in the drama, for Weiss's
pseudohistorical world pretends the actually committed Sade
and Marat were fellow inmates at the asylum. Sade relates the
fictional experience which was responsible for his incarceration:
in an Artaudian display of cruelty, he had acted out his fantasies
and, like Genet's brothel patrons, was purged of their effects; no
longer did he wish violence in life; no longer did he encourage
revolution. Ironically, in the eyes of the world this was madness,
and Sade was committed to the asylum, where he now indulges
in art as therapy.

Yet the very form of Weiss's drama reflects the possibility—as does Weiss's own political choice—that the author's
search was not for an individual self so much as for a place
among others. Marat/Sade employs many of the methods of
Brechtian drama, including episodic structure and alienation effects. Its concern with the communal operation of man is reflected not only by the philosophy of the revolution, but by the
artistic efforts of the asylum inmates. That we may be nothing
more than social role is suggested by Weiss's choice of specific
inmates for specific roles. Ruby Cohn points to Duperret and Corday as examples of the oneness of identity and role:

Duperret and Charlotte Corday are played by an erotomanic and a somnambulist, and their illnesses intrude upon their fictional roles. When Duperret meets Corday—"nobility meets grace"— idealism is undercut by the stumbling somnambulism of the one and the compulsive eroticism of the other.[8]

Even more strongly supportive of this suggestion are the play's repeated strippings away of illusion to reveal not reality but only another illusion. And, finally, the play's fusion of painting and drama—the momentary freezing of Corday, poised with dagger in hand, into a tableau as the chorus quickly runs through fifteen years of history, and Marat's death pose, precisely the position in which he has been immortalized by David's painting—offers the most visual suggestion that all is role.

On September 1, 1965, the Stockholm newspaper, *Dagens Nyheter*, carried Weiss's announcement:

In the two possible choices remaining to me today I see only in the socialist ordered society the possibility of removing the existing disproportions in the world . . . my work can only be fruitful if it stands in direct relation to those forces which signify for me the positive strength of this world.[9]

Weiss may have resolved the dialectic for himself, but in *Marat/Sade* the archetypal reality of subconscious impulses and desires is never completely reconciled with the social role, leaving not only the political question but the question of the self unresolved.

Artistically, however, the survival of the metafictional character confirms the fact that the inmates of Charenton are abnormal in more than psychological terms. Collectively they are Weiss's attempt at creating characters who go beyond psychological realism to fulfill that conception of theater suggested by Artaud in his letters on language:

We need true action, but without practical consequence. It is not on the social level that the action of theater unfolds. Still less on the ethical and psychological levels. . . . This obstinacy in making characters talk about feelings, passions, desires, and impulses of a strictly psychological order, in which a single word is to compensate for innumerable gestures, is the reason . . . the theater has lost its true *raison d'être*.[10]

The combined and continuing fact of Weiss's mad actors' reality and their roles creates a simultaneous presence of irrationality and rationality which cannot be reconciled in psychological terms. But as Susan Sontag points out:

> By combining rational or near-rational argument with irrational behavior, Weiss is not inviting the audience to make a judgment on Sade's [or the other's] character, mental competence, or state of mind. Rather, he is shifting to a kind of theater focused not on characters, but on intense transpersonal emotions borne by characters. He is providing a kind of vicarious emotional experience (in this case, frankly erotic) from which the theater has shied away too long.[11]

One can readily understand how Geraldine Lust, speaking at the *Marat/Sade* Forum, could call the play "a primer for the kind of theatre to come,"

> a harbinger of plays that will reflect the human condition at its core. These plays will reveal the psychology underlying our myths and societies, rather than be a narrow description of individual behavior.[12]

As art, Weiss's play is clearly as revolutionary as Marat's ideals. The sustained multiplicity of the metafictional character simultaneously affirms and disrupts the conventional orientation of a play's inherent dialectic. It creates a situation in which 1793, 1808, 1949, 1964, and, indeed, the year of any subsequent performance, can simultaneously exist. It creates a freedom of movement in time and space while simultaneously reaffirming the confines of art: deferring to the mimetic quality of art, Weiss does not permit Corday to murder Marat until she has knocked three times, yet, defying that same premise, he freezes her in the death-delivering pose as the chorus catalogues fifteen years of historical events. In that tableau Weiss succeeds in telescoping time, moving from the dramatized murder to the actual murder and back again. And it suggests, finally, that the art of madmen may be our only definition of reality.

✠Five
Albee's Martha and George

AS JOSEPH WOOD KRUTCH points out in his study, *"Modernism" in Modern Drama*,[1] "modern drama" began late in America. It was not until the 1920s—well into Shaw's long and prolific career as a writer, and a decade after the death of Ibsen, whose drama had already been popular for twenty-five years—that America's "first modern playwright," Eugene O'Neill, became established as a significant dramatic voice.

O'Neill's modernity, however, was mostly on the surface, and for the most part his plays (despite the ponderous experimental works) continued the realistic tradition in American drama. In fact, except for a period of expressionism in the 1930s, realistic drama persisted, unchallenged, in America for an unduly long period of time. As C. W. E. Bigsby observes in his excellent study of the American theatre, *Confrontation and Commitment:*

> America had remained strangely insulated not only from the European revolt against the well-made-play but also from its rejection of a drama of resolution and reassurance. Certainly at the very time when European dramatists were turning away from psychology and sociology the American theatre was producing plays like *Tea and Sympathy* (1953), *Cat on a Hot Tin Roof* (1955) and *A View from the Bridge* (1955).[2]

It was not until 1959, when Jack Gelber's *The Connection* was produced in New York, that the American theater became introspective and began its own self-evaluation. Bigsby, in fact, cites *The Connection* as the philosophical fulcrum between the plays of O'Neill and Williams and those of Albee and the later Miller. But he sees as even more significant the fact that *The Connection* was virtually the first American play which, like Pirandello's *Six Characters*, asked the question, What is drama?

> *The Connection* did potentially for American drama what Pirandello had done for Italian and indeed European drama as a whole. It dismissed a form which had ceased to serve the theatre and the purpose of drama.[3]

With Gelber, realism in American drama began feeling the effects of "the other tradition":

> . . . the dominant theme of contemporary American drama is that embodied in the work of Gelber, Albee and the late Miller. The need to confront reality . . . is expressed in all the major drama of the United States since 1959. This movement, which constitutes an end to revolt, has been accompanied by an increasing artistic self-awareness so that these last years have produced a greater and more original re-assessment of the nature of the dramatic process than has ever been the case before in America.[4]

Among the most important figures in American drama, and surely the dominant American playwright of the early 1960s, is Edward Albee. His best-known play, *Who's Afraid of Virginia Woolf?* had its first Broadway run at the Billy Rose Theatre in the 1962–63 season, and, despite some reviewers' disgust over its vulgarity and viciousness,[5] the play quickly acquired status as a masterpiece of the American theater. Out of the proliferation of critical attention have come interpretations of the play as an allegory of the American dream, an example of the cosmic yearning of the female principle of creation for the civilizing influence of the masculine, a dramatization of a couple's coming of age, a depiction of a homosexual liaison, a parody of the Mass of Requiem, and an examination into the horrors of a science-dominated world.[6] The one thematic overlay, however, which persists in this play and throughout the work of Albee, is the relationship between reality and illusion. *Who's Afraid of Virginia Woolf?* is informed with a continuing sense of those concerns which Bigsby has called characteristic of the contemporary American theater: man's "need to confront reality" and "artistic self-awareness."

In Albee's play, George and Martha are double characters. They acquire their duality by virtue of a self-created fantasy world, at the center of which is an imaginary son. The couple, unable to produce biological offspring, have managed to preserve their twenty-three-year-old marriage through pretending to themselves that a son exists, inventing all the appropriate childhood stories to support their illusion. The pair live two existences, one as a couple who cannot have children—their "real" identities—and the other, more private existence as parents of a now twenty-one-year-old son—their fictive identities.

Through the duality of his central characters, Albee probes into the question of a man's need to confront reality. In a world where reality itself or the many collective constructs of mankind no longer offer meaning, are man's private constructs of alternate realities justifiable? In Who's Afraid of Virginia Woolf? one must consider whether the fantasies of George and Martha are, as Richard Schechner calls them, the manifestation of an "ineluctable urge to escape reality and its concomitant responsibilities by crawling back into the womb, or bathroom, or both," [7] or whether they are, indeed, a meaningful confrontation of reality.

Throughout the play it is obvious that George and Martha's marriage is less than ideal. George, living in the shadow of Martha's college president father, is a somewhat unspectacular history professor, who was the only man in his department the army did not take and who could rank as department chairman only when the others were away at war. He is a man who in the past saw the deaths of both his parents and who still lives under the burden of responsibility. In addition to his guilt-ridden conscience, he must live with the continual taunts of his wife, who thrives on reminding her husband of the strength of her personality and the impotence of his. Martha, frustrated by being trapped in a small college town with a dull husband, finds her chief frustration in the fact that they are childless. The two incessantly and mercilessly indulge themselves in a sadomasochistic relationship, destroying each other continually with verbal, and sometimes physical, abuse. It is this ugly and unbearable reality from which George and Martha seek refuge in their illusion.

Is Albee, then, affirming the private constructs of man? Is he suggesting that rather than confronting a reality on terms which he cannot understand, man should confront an alternate reality of his own creation? After all, as Richard E. Amacher observes, "George and Martha were probably happier while under the influence of the illusion."[8] Despite this speculation, however, it is quite clear from the play's ending that Lawrence Kingsley is correct in noting:

> Albee introduces illusion only to reassess it, to show how his characters must rid themselves of falsehood and return to the world in which they must live.[9]

This statement is particularly well borne out when we consider the condition of George and Martha's doubleness at the end of the play. The couple who, with a "hint of communion,"[10] accept joint responsibility for their sterile marriage ("We couldn't [have children]" [p. 238]) and prepare to face "Sunday tomorrow, all day" (p. 239), are nakedly the "real" George and Martha. When George murders their fictive son by arranging an imaginary car crash on the boy's twenty-first birthdy, he just as certainly murders the fictive portion of his and Martha's identities. Also killed in that crash are the parents of the unfortunate lad.

In fact, the play has slowly but inexorably been leading to the death of the parents.[11] The gradually revealed story of the murder of George's own parents is not in the play simply to justify George's guilt. George may well have been the boy who at fifteen shot his mother, at sixteen crashed his car into a tree, killing his father, and for the thirty years since has been in an "asylum" (George's life with Martha), not uttering a word (pp. 94–96). But if George did not murder his parents then, he surely murders parents at the end of the play. The story, whether fact or not, is an anticipation (as is the shotgun George earlier aimed at Martha) of that climactic event, a parallel to George's ultimate destruction of his and Martha's fictive identities. The final scene, then, sees a triple death: that of the fictive son, that of the fictive parents, and that of fiction itself.

Albee is far from affirming illusion as a way of life. The fact that there is a discernible—and recoverable—real self, when the layers of game play and fantasy are stripped from George and Martha, supports Albee's commitment to man's need to confront reality on *its* terms. Yet Albee does not without qualification decry the evils of illusion. Although ostensibly a realistic drama, *Who's Afraid of Virginia Woolf?* is supremely aware of itself as a play and manifests this awareness throughout. Where the illusion of George and Martha is dismissed as an unsatisfactory confrontation of reality, the illusion of their creator, Albee himself—i.e., the play—is upheld as a meaningful creation, for the play, unlike the escapist illusion of its central characters, leads toward truth rather than away from it.

That Albee is concerned not only with the relationship between reality and illusion with repect to patterns of life, but with the artistic process as well, is confirmed by an examination of the relationship between George and Martha on the one hand and Nick and Honey, their youthful guests, on the other, for this relationship is a microcosm of the relationship betwen play and audience and a statement of the positive function of art.

What differentiates the specific destructive occasion dramatized by *Who's Afraid of Virginia Woolf?* from all the other nights of game playing George and Martha, by implication, have experienced, is the fact that the couple has an audience. When George hears that he and Martha are to have late-night visitors, he is quick to direct Martha not to "start on the bit" (p. 18), the "bit" being conversation about their son. But when Martha and Honey return from their trip to the "euphemism," it is clear that Martha has indeed revealed their secret. In so doing she has defied what has been an inviolate rule: she has turned their private game of "sonny boy" into a public one. Nick and Honey become not only the means of a group therapy session, but, in an artistic sense, they become audience, with George and Martha the performers.

Although George and Martha have had audiences before

("Anybody who comes here ends up getting . . . testy" [p. 99]),
they have avoided playing the game of their son, for that game is
for their own private benefit. This night, though, Martha brings
up the son, and as George faces each new defeat that Martha
inflicts upon him, the game becomes more intense, until it culminates in George's murder of both the boy and the parents. The
fact that an audience is present is largely responsible for the exorcism, for it is through Nick and Honey's involvement that
George is able to effect purgation and Albee is able to affirm both
the mimetic and purgative effects of art.

As Nick and Honey play audience to the performance of
George and Martha, similarities between the two couples become
apparent. The fathers of both Honey and Martha are god-figures,
Honey's being a minister and Martha's the college president,
whom she worships. Just as George and Martha created an imaginary child through which they sustain their marriage, so Honey
created an hysterical pregnancy, through which she established
her marriage. Just as the "bergin" boy (George?) murdered, so
does Honey, in George's terms, murder through various means of
preventing conception, or perhaps even through abortion ("How
do you make your secret little murders stud-boy doesn't know
about, hunh? Pills? . . . Apple jelly? WILL POWER?" [p. 177]).
The narcissistic reflection each couple finds in the other is a
comment on the mimetic relationship of play and audience. Nick
and Honey (the audience) see in George and Martha (the performers) the truth of their own experience.

The purgative operation of art is seen through both artist
and audience. The paradox of the artistic process—that creative
genius, being subconscious, experiences the destruction of its
very nature when externalized—is dramatized by George and
Martha's conversion of their private game into a public one and
the consequent death of their illusion. But the purgation exists
for audience as well as creator, for once externalized as art, the
creative genius is capable of affecting others. George and
Martha's play seriously touches Nick and Honey. When the
younger couple leave the house, Honey has discarded her fears
of motherhood and Nick is convinced that now he understands.

Both artist and audience, purged of illusion, stand drained, with at least the potential if not the promise of renewal. Artistically as well as psychologically, purgation is achieved for both couples.

So intent is Albee upon examining the nature of his own creation that he uses an alterego within the world of the play. George, in addition to the duality of character which he and Martha share, also possesses a distinct identity as playwright-director. In much the same way Lionel Abel[12] views Hamlet, or Josephine Bennett[13] views the duke in *Measure for Measure,* Albee endows his central character with yet another double identity: George is both a character in the play and a detached representation of the playwright as artist and director.

As a character, George is psychologically beaten by Martha's venomous tongue and dominant personality, but as artist-director, he is very much in control. In fact, there is no evidence that George as character ever desired to be a parent, and his fictive identity as father may well be the product of his status as artist-director, assumed purely for its manipulative benefits with respect to Martha. When, upon George's announcement of the death of their son, Martha cries, "NO! NO! YOU CANNOT DO THAT! YOU CAN'T DECIDE THAT FOR YOURSELF! I WILL NOT LET YOU DO THAT!" (p. 232), George retorts, "YOU KNOW THE RULES, MARTHA! . . . I can kill him, Martha, if I want to" (p. 235). Repeatedly George returns to their illusion, the one area over which he has absolute control, to defeat Martha.

In Act I, for example, when Martha reveals the story of the boxing incident, George is enraged to the point of tears and bottle breaking, but he is out of control only momentarily. He retaliates by aiming the shotgun (which proves to be only a toy, a stage prop) at Martha, and when he regains control he brings up the issue of their son, forcing Martha to tell their guests when the boy is coming home.

In Act II the balance tips back to Martha, who regains control by telling the story of George's novel. Her father had read the story about a boy who killed his parents and was told by George that it was not fiction but fact. George is humiliated and again infuriated by this revelation, and this time tries to strangle Martha.

But the act ends with George plotting revenge again through his son: he is rehearsing the news that their son is dead.

While Martha is thoroughly involved emotionally with their creation, George, as artist-director, maintains a distance from the boy, using him as a means of pandering to Martha's frustrations and gaining control over a woman who by nature is the stronger force in their marriage. Following each emotional involvement which George as character experiences, George as artist-director grabs hold of the strings that control him and Martha, the myth of their son. In an essay entitled "Language: Truth and Illusion in Who's Afraid of Virginia Woolf?" Ruth Meyer notes: "Although Martha considers herself the Earth Mother . . . it is George who is the Creative Force in the play."[14] Actually, George as artist-director is more than the "Creative Force": he is creator, controller, and destroyer.

Significantly, the destruction of Martha and George's illusion is a decision which is exclusively George's. As artist-director, it is essential to him that he remain detached, keeping reality and illusion separate. In the Walpurgisnacht act, however, he momentarily loses touch with reality, for it is then that Martha reveals to George who it is who drinks "bergin," thus causing the narrative of George's friend to become the story of George. But this same story had already been transformed into fiction in the form of George's novel and restored to truth by Martha's father's recognition of it as fact. When the multiple perceptions of this event converge, reality and fiction become indistinct even for George, and it is at that point that he decides he must end the illusion. For if he is unable to distinguish between the real and the fictive, he can no longer be in control. Similarly, in the third act, "The Exorcism," it is Martha's taunts relating to Nick's being a houseboy or a stud—"Truth and illusion, George, you don't know the difference" (p. 202)—which cause the whole thing to snap. Without hesitation, George announces they've one more game to play, "bringing up baby."

From the point of that decision, George's detachment grows, affecting even the character George. He can directly and unemotionally confront Martha and Nick following their escapade in the kitchen at 4 A.M.; he can retreat into intellectualizing about "the West encumbered by crippling alliances and burdened with a morality too rigid to accommodate itself to the swing of events, [which] must eventually fall" (p. 174) (foreshadowing the climactic scene); he can speak in a falsetto voice, strew flowers, and mistake Nick for Sonny—all in the contrived manner of an actor who is self-consciously remaining apart from the role he is playing.

What emerges from George's dual identity as character and artist-director is a dramatization of the artistic process itself, through which Albee affirms art as an acceptable—and, indeed, redeeming—form of illusion. While it is clear that the games of George and Martha are attempts to avoid reality, it is also clear that games, when formalized into art, are not simply escapism. For while Albee does not sanction illusion as a way of life, he does uphold the play itself as a form of illusion which ultimately leads toward truth.

Albee's metafictional characters, then, simultaneously deny the validity of illusion as a way of life and affirm the validity of illusion as art. Albee asks his audience to enter a world of illusion only as a means of discovery, because for Albee, the function of fiction, whether private or public, is to illuminate, not replace, reality.

♪Six

Stoppard's Moon and Birdboot,
Rosencrantz and Guildenstern

WHAT ALLARDYCE NICOLL calls the "fourth movement" in modern English drama began on May 8, 1956 at the Royal Court Theatre, when John Osborne's *Look Back in Anger* opened.[1] The performance, commonly accepted as a landmark in British theatrical history, began the revitalization of a theater somewhat stagnated by classical revivals, musicals, and realistic social plays. John Russell Taylor, in his influential book, *The Angry Theatre,* characterizes the event:

> Although . . . "the Osborne generation" proved only the first of several waves, 8 May 1956 still marks the real breakthrough of "the new drama" into the British theatre, and Osborne himself remains, one way and another, one of its most influential exponents, as well as representing for the general public the new dramatist *par excellence,* the first of the angry young men and arguably the biggest shock to the system of the British theatre since the advent of Shaw.[2]

In fact, Taylor even suggests that Osborne's play was responsible for preventing the absolute entrenchment of the novel as the supreme form of literary expression in England.[3]

While it is difficult to assess the tangential effects of the Osborne play, or, even at this point, the endurance of its impact on the history of drama, surely *Look Back in Anger* marked the beginning of a line of experimental theater in England which was to be continued and developed by such new playwrights as John Arden, N. F. Simpson, Harold Pinter, Edward Bond, David Storey, Peter Shaffer, and Tom Stoppard. Though Osborne's drama was unconventional in terms of its content—its capturing, through character and language, of the moral and metaphysical outrage of a generation—much of the drama which followed was to raise its voice in protest over the very form of drama. The plays of Tom Stoppard are just such plays.

Along with Harold Pinter, Tom Stoppard is probably the most important playwright on the contemporary British scene. His plays, like those of Pinter, are informed with a tragicomic sense of the absurd and the contingent nature of man's existence. A frequently recurring character in Stoppard's plays is the marginal man, the character standing on the fringe of the central action, tentatively placing first one foot and then the other into the arena of activity. Speaking of Stoppard's first and best-known play, *Rosencrantz and Guildenstern Are Dead* (1966), C. W. E. Bigsby characterizes Stoppard's vision of man:

> Man, in other words, is a minor character in a drama which he cannot understand, dependent for recognition on people who do not even control their own fate and forces which may not even exist.[4]

Man's confrontation with his world is a recurring theme in Stoppard's plays. Whether rendered in the form of two minor characters from a Shakespearean play assuming heroic status (*Rosencrantz and Guildenstern Are Dead*), a professor of moral philosophy discoursing on God while his ex-showgirl wife plays surrealistic games (*Jumpers*, 1972), or a pseudohistorical meeting in a Zurich library of three radically different revolutionaries, Lenin, Joyce, and Tristan Tzara (*Travesties*, 1974), the theme of man's relationship to reality—his insignificance, exile, and search for self—is manifest.

As important as Stoppard's philosophical explorations, however, is his preoccupation with his own art. Stoppard's plays are nonrealistic in form, undisguisedly theatrical, and supremely self-conscious. Indeed, the playwright has succeeded admirably in uniting the innovative form of his plays with their philosophical content, making his ventures into the nature of reality—and illusion—inquiries into the very rationale for art. One of Stoppard's less well-known plays, The Real Inspector Hound, which premièred in London in 1968, is a particularly fine example of how a playwright integrates these concerns through the use of a metafictional character.

Like the characters of each of the playwrights studied thus far, Stoppard's characters acquire metafictional status by virtue of play within play. In the case of The Real Inspector Hound, this "play" is formalized into a structural demand. The characters, who are made to function within two structural units, acquire one identity in the frame play—their "real" identities—and quite another in the inner play—their fictive identities. But the distinction between the identities, and, indeed, between the plays, remains less than absolute. As the characters move across the boundary that separates the outer play from the inner one, the line which separates their identities as critics and members of an audience from their identities as actors and participants in the "whodunit" play becomes increasingly fluid, as does the line which separates the reality of their world as audience and the fiction of the world of Muldoon Manor. In creating first a rigid structural line of demarcation and then violating that line through his protagonists' entrance into the inner play, Stoppard is able to use the play-within-a-play not simply in the traditional way, for enhancing reality, but rather to suggest the nature of role playing and the power of illusion over reality.

The setting for The Real Inspector Hound is an unusually clever one. Besides the seating area for audience and the playing area for actors, there is a third locale in Stoppard's theatre: rows of seats—or the impression of such seats—face the audience, with the stage between the real audience and the fictive one. Moon and Birdboot, Stoppard's fictive critics, position themselves in the front row of these seats among the fictive audience. Through this setting, Stoppard is honoring (if only playfully) the classical concept of art imitating nature—the audience is face to face not only with a stage, but with itself. And he is also suggesting, paradoxically, the mirror as a symbol of illusion.

Our initial response to Moon and Birdboot (before the play-within-a-play begins) is amused self-recognition. We watch Moon mimic typical preplay audience gestures: staring blankly ahead, turning his head from side to side as though waiting for someone, and flipping through the pages of his program. When Birdboot joins him, we recognize their conversation as being singularly like our own: they discuss personal matters and professional matters, all on the superficial level permitted by the limited time allowed for preplay patter. The verisimilitude is convincing and works in a conventional way to create a sense of identification between the audience and the critics, but it is in the relationship of Moon and Birdboot to the play-within-a-play that their "reality" is established.

When the play-within-a-play begins, the way in which we view Moon and Birdboot instantly changes. While their identities to this point are those of actors in a mimetic play, when Mrs. Drudge walks on the stage between the critics and audience and begins the Muldoon Manor play, Moon and Birdboot are no longer simply fictive characters. In the presence of Mrs. Drudge, we find ourselves making a distinction between the status of the housekeeper and that of the critics, and as she and the inhabitants of Muldoon Manor take us deeper into the fictionalized world of the play-within-a-play, we increasingly tend to view the frame play, which consists of the conversations of Moon and Birdboot, as an extension of our own reality rather than as play (a process which is once removed from the very experience inherent in the audience/play relationship and to which we are being simultaneously subjected). In fact, we allow Moon and Birdboot virtually to lose their fictionalized status by repeatedly looking to them for their reactions.

As the play-within-a-play continues, we listen to the personal and critical remarks of Moon and Birdboot which Stoppard has cleverly used to intercut and punctuate the acts of the Muldoon Manor play, forcing us to maintain consciously a clear mental line between the world of Muldoon Manor and the "real" world of the critics. Ironically, Stoppard makes no attempt to disguise the fact that Moon and Birdboot are indeed participants in a play; the critics readily admit that the play *has* started *before* anyone has appeared on the Muldoon Manor set. But this, of course, is Stoppard's way of enjoying a private joke, knowing as he does that within moments Mrs. Drudge, clearly a fictional character, will appear to authenticate the critics' reality.

The clear mental line we have established, however, is only temporarily secure. Through the creation of two separate plays, Stoppard manipulates his audience into a compartmentalizing of characters; once the dichotomy of play world and "nonplay" world is established, he proceeds to upset any certainty with respect to those worlds by integrating the plays. Any clear sense we may have had of what is "real" and what is "fictive" is almost irrecoverably disturbed when Moon and Birdboot step forward into Mrs. Muldoon's drawing room and become double characters.

There is a comment made by Moon—almost in passing—between Acts I and II of the "whodunit" play, which at that point seems inappropriate: he says the play is about "the nature of identity." The less than subtle exposition of that play (itself a parody of countless detective tales in which several characters establish their motives for wishing the victim dead) has given Moon little cause to make such a statement, even allowing for his pretentions to intellectualism. Stoppard, however, has every reason to make the remark, and, as an authorial statement, the remark refers not simply to the Muldoon Manor play, but to the entire play. Through the physical interaction between the "real" characters of the outer play and the fictive characters of the inner play, Stoppard is indeed setting up a commentary on the nature of identity.

Part of the conversation of Moon and Birdboot before the beginning of the inner play concerns Birdboot's previous evening's activities. He had spent the evening with an actress who is—not coincidentally—to appear in the play the critics are there to see. Our placement of that circumstance is, naturally enough, removed from the theater; we accept the meeting as having been part of the nonplay world of Birdboot. Similarly, when Birdboot reacts to the beauty of the actress playing Cynthia Muldoon, we place that circumstance as clearly part of that same world. We do not yet make the connection between the events of the nonplay world and the events of the play world. It is only in retrospect, as the play and its surprises unfold, that the exact parallel in the situations of Birdboot and the fictive Simon Gascoyne emerge: just as Birdboot spent the evening with the actress playing Felicity and is now ready to abandon her for the actress playing Cynthia, so did Simon spend the evening with Felicity and is now ready to abandon her for Cynthia.

But more than mimesis is occurring.

The double characters which Moon and Birdboot are to become are anticipated by the dichotomy embodied in this parallel, i.e., that every character has both a real and a fictive identity, the fictive identity being manifested through roles. In much the same way as Pirandello's father and daughter reenact the brothel scene in *Six Characters* and then watch the actors reenact their reenactment, Stoppard here creates a "real" situation and then assigns actors to play out that situation. We as audience have no difficulty in seeing Birdboot's situation as "real" and Simon Gascoyne's as fictive—until Birdboot unwittingly becomes involved in the fictive action, at which point the role and the "real" merge, seemingly inextricably.

When the Muldoon Manor telephone rings between acts with a call from Birdboot's wife, the critic relinquishes his seat and steps onto the stage. And when Felicity's tennis ball flies through the open window, followed by Felicity, Birdboot becomes—through the unwitting assumption of that role—Simon Gascoyne. The adjustment is no easier for an audience to make than it is for Birdboot. We find ourselves first attempting to reject Birdboot as Simon and to make an adjustment in our perception of Felicity, relinquishing our concept of her as a character in a play and accepting her instead as the woman with whom Birdboot spent last evening. But such a perception cannot sustain itself when Felicity persists in repeating the lines earlier spoken by her to Simon. The fictive Felicity, in control of our perceptions, draws us back, along with Birdboot, into the fictive world. Despite his unwillingness to assume the role and our insistence on still seeing him as critic, Birdboot has become the incarnation of his role, a role which was earlier represented by a fictive character. As critic and Simon Gascoyne, Birdboot has become a double character.

Moon, as yet still a spectator, sees the extent of Birdboot's involvement and attempts to persuade his partner to return to his seat. He is unable, however, to prevent the inevitable consequences of the Muldoon Manor plot: since Birdboot is now Simon, he must be killed. As Moon rushes onstage to retrieve Birdboot, a shot rings out, and Birdboot falls dead. But like his partner before him, by stepping into the Muldoon Manor drawing room, Moon relinquishes more than just his seat; the moment he intrudes upon the fictive world, his identity loses its singularity. With Cynthia's entrance, Moon finds himself caught in a situation just as inescapable as Birdboot's: he has become "Inspector Hound." And, as was the case with his partner, the consequences of that role are inevitable: script has become destiny,[5] and Moon is powerless to prevent the accusation of murder or his ensuing death.

The Real Inspector Hound is, indeed, about "the nature of identity," its central concern being that of a functional or role-playing self. The plight of the critics is reminiscent of our own acquiescence to the demands of social convention, which constantly force us to assume a fictive identity and may result in the essential self's becoming indistinguishable from the role. The remark of the jealous Moon with respect to Higgs, the critic for whom he will always be a stand-in, is an appropriate comment on the double self which develops in the play: "my presence defines his absence, his absence confirms my presence, his presence precludes mine" (p. 9). Moon and Higgs are actually present simultaneously (the dead body turns out to be Higgs), but not in their roles as critics. And the two identities which Moon and Birdboot each possesses exist simultaneously, but when the fictive side of those identities is in operation, the real side cannot be acknowledged. Like actors who assume the part imposed upon them, the individual, by assuming social roles, is sacrificing his essential self.

The final irony of Stoppard's play is that Moon's understudy, Puckeridge, is the mastermind of the confusion. Just as Moon had dreamed of killing Higgs, envisioning a world in which actors are slaughtered by their understudies, magicians sawn in half by glamour girls, and superiors destroyed by their subordinates,[6] so Puckeridge dreamed of an identity independent of Moon, for whom he was an understudy. But Puckeridge realized his dream. In a dramatic insistence upon defining his own identity, Puckeridge arranges—through the very medium which he, Moon, and Higgs criticize—the murder of his superiors.

The end of the play sees a mass interchange of identities: Birdboot's body replaces that of Simon Gascoyne, Moon's replaces that of the murder victim (who is actually Higgs); the actors who played Simon Gascoyne and Inspector Hound step outside the Muldoon Manor drawing room to occupy the seats formerly occupied by Birdboot and Moon and begin making critical remarks about the whodunit play. Now Moon's earlier remark that the play has started and that this is just a pause becomes meaningful. The play is an endless cycle in which two actors—who are, after all, fictive—begin as observers and assume roles within the play they are watching until the line between their reality and the fiction no longer exists. Just as the whodunit play had earlier served to authenticate the critics' reality, now it serves to betray it. Once the fictionalized reality of Moon and Birdboot has become pure fiction, the play, despite its cyclic nature, must end. The audience cannot view the next cycle, since it cannot now accept the two men in the critics' seats as real, and the play depends completely upon that acceptance. In order for the play to continue there must be a new audience, and the line between reality and fiction must again be established.

But Stoppard's play is not only about identity, it is about art as well. The dichotomy between the real and the fictive self which his metafictional characters embody extends as well to the relationship between art and reality.

Stoppard's use of the play-within-a-play structure is in one respect like Shakespeare's use of the device in *Hamlet*: the inner play does indeed fulfill the purpose of art, which is to hold a mirror up to nature. The experience of Birdboot (who is audience) is faithfully duplicated in the inner play. But Stoppard originally told us that his mirror image was "impossible," and his fidelity to the mimetic theory ends with this token honoring.

In fact, art emerges in *The Real Inspector Hound* as a force capable of controlling reality. The inner play in *Hamlet* is able to affect reality only to the extent of the recognition of its audience (Claudius) of the similarity between fiction and reality. Stoppard sets up the play-within-a-play structure so that the distinction between reality and illusion is established, but the distinction is made only so that it might be destroyed. By the end of *The Real Inspector Hound,* the inner play breaks through the boundary separating it from the outer play and encompasses the outer play. In mimetic art, illusion may, in a sense, be said to be giving up its identity, trying to pass for reality. In Stoppard's art, illusion is autonomous. When the inner play breaks through its boundary, illusion imposes itself upon reality, in essence destroying the right of reality to be separately defined. And, as we have seen, the power of illusion is complete: the frame play can no longer be accepted as "reality"; the critics can now be nothing but fictionalized characters. Nor does the power of illusion stop once it has destroyed the reality of the outer play. It extends to our own reality, which is reflected in the reality of the critics, destroying that as well. And if the mirror which reflected our reality is illusion, then perhaps reality *is* illusion after all.

In Stoppard's earlier play, *Rosencrantz and Guildenstern Are Dead,* a similar set of first marginally involved and then seriously involved characters exists. Every bit as unperceptive as their counterparts in *Inspector Hound,* Rosencrantz and Guildenstern become victims of the play, which defines and controls them. Though philosophically consistent and structurally similar, however, the two plays are hardly carbon copies.

Rosencrantz and Guildenstern Are Dead was first performed as part of the "fringe" of the Edinburgh Festival in 1966. Its first professional performance was in London at the Old Vic, where it opened in 1967; its New York première took place six months later. Reviews were enthusiastic though mixed, John Simon calling the play a "conception of genius" reduced to a "tour de force."[7] As virtually all reviewers noticed, *Rosencrantz and Guildenstern* was clearly derivative, constructed of passages of poetry from Shakespeare (*Hamlet*) and rather loud echoes of Pirandello (*Six Characters*) and Beckett (*Waiting for Godot*). Despite being what Robert Brustein called a "theatrical parasite,"[8] however, the play possesses indisputable originality, particularly in the way in which Rosencrantz and Guildenstern achieve their own unique status as metafictional characters.

Though levity is characteristic of most of Stoppard's plays, as we have seen in *The Real Inspector Hound*, that lightness is frequently a surface quality under which more serious concerns lie. Surely this is the case with *Rosencrantz and Guildenstern*, which may be every bit as sober a play philosophically as Beckett's *Waiting for Godot*. In fact, like Didi and Gogo, Rosencrantz and Guildenstern experience the desperation of knowing they must amuse themselves continually in order to pass the time. Like the tramps, the two involve themselves in verbal games and vaudeville routines, and indulge in a kind of self-congratulation for their efforts. A decade and a half removed from their tramp predecessors, however, Rosencrantz and Guildenstern occupy a world in which the questions have changed to premises. The arbitrary quality of the universe which puzzles Vladimir to frustration is a donnée of Rosencrantz and Guildenstern's world, in which even the laws of chance no longer exist: the two flip a coin ninety-two times and watch it turn up heads each time, the unbewildered Rosencrantz experiencing only embarrassment at having won all of Guildenstern's coins. Far from searching for significance in the macrocosm, Rosencrantz and Guildenstern care only about affirming the significance of their own little lives. As Rosencrantz says, "We don't question, we don't doubt. We perform."[9] It is the fact of this performance which is at the heart of Stoppard's investigation into the play's more serious concerns.

Structurally, Stoppard uses a variation of the play-within-a-play to create his characters' metafictional status. The outer play is the ordinary world of Rosencrantz and Guildenstern, a world characterized by coin flipping, game playing, and philosophical discussions on the nature of death. The inner play is *Hamlet*, or scenes from *Hamlet*, which the audience immediately recognizes as it witnesses the meeting between Ophelia and Hamlet, which begins the inner action. Our experience with metafictional characters in a play-within-a-play structure tells us to view the coin flippers, the occupants of the frame play, as "real" and Hamlet's spy friends, the occupants of the inner play, as fictive. But the fact that these characters have an existence which precedes the Stoppard play alters this. Surely Rosencrantz and Guildenstern, though speaking in a modern tongue inappropriate to their Elizabethan garb, can be none other than Shakespeare's ill-fated pair. The fact is that the characters' dramatic existence does not begin with Act I of the Stoppard play; the characters have an inseparable preexistence which significantly affects our response. Though we are aware of the duality, we cannot with comfort divide the metafictional characters into the fictive and the real, for we cannot consider the coin flippers "real" without being haunted by their preexistence. Even before Hamlet appears, then, we are thinking of Rosencrantz and Guildenstern in relation to him, and even before the two become reintegrated into the *Hamlet* play, we are aware of their fate, for our knowledge of Shakespeare, as well as the title of the play, tells us that Rosencrantz and Guildenstern are dead.

Whether we view the inner play or the outer play as Rosencrantz and Guildenstern's real world, however, is not so important as the fact which Stoppard reveals in endowing his characters with literary preexistence. Rosencrantz and Guildenstern may well exemplify Sartre's existential premise, but for them the essence which precedes existence is itself fictive, reducing (or elevating) the status of these two to pure fiction. Indeed, the theatrical metaphor which sustains itself throughout the play underscores the playwright's vision of life as essentially dramatic and of living as nothing more than playing a role. When in the outer play, Stoppard's characters exist through self-created dramas, which increase in emotional intensity as the repartee reaches its climax. Once they are reminded of *Hamlet*, they dramatize their meeting with the young prince as it occurred in Shakespeare, but before it occurs in the inner play, and dramatize their meeting with the English king, which occurred only by implication in *Hamlet*. These dramatic presentations, however, are invariably inadequate, for while they characterize the dramatic quality of Rosencrantz and Guildenstern's lives, they are only a prelude to the more fulfilling roles for which the Shakespeare play predestines them. It is only when Rosencrantz and Guildenstern step fully into the *Hamlet* play and resume their roles without resistance that they realize their sole raison d'être *is* those roles.

While Rosencrantz and Guildenstern may be unaware of the power of play, there is one character in the play who is supremely aware of it, and that is the Player, head of the travelling tragedians who act out *The Murder of Gonzago*. Strongly reminiscent of Pirandello's *Six Characters*, these actors never change out of their costumes, are always in character, always *on*, roaming the countryside in search of an audience. As the Player explains, "We're actors. . . . We pledged our identities, secure in the conventions of our trade, that someone would be watching" (p. 64). As purely fictional characters, defined by their roles, they are distinguished from Rosencrantz and Guildenstern by their knowledge that they exist only within a script. When Guildenstern naively asks the Player who decides who dies in their tragedies, the surprised Player replies, "Decides? It is *written*" (p. 80). And it is Rosencrantz's turn to be surprised when the Player tells him what happens to old actors: "Nothing. They're still acting" (p. 115).

Despite the presence of the players, Rosencrantz and Guildenstern do not fully understand what is happening, nor why, yet by the end of the play they have reconciled themselves to their fate and, indeed, even affirmed it. Befuddlement characterizes the two from the moment they replace the figures in the dumb show who wear their costumes through the moment they read the letter condemning them to sudden death. Rosencrantz, in fact, is even a bit scared and, watching the early stages of the *Hamlet* play, tries to convince Guildenstern that they should leave. Guildenstern, appearing to be the more aware of the two, seems to realize that even though their roles in the *Hamlet* play are minor ones, their dramatic existence—indeed, their *existence*—depends on them, and he convinces Rosencrantz that they must remain. Once their fate is sealed, Rosencrantz too stops resisting, even acknowledging, "To tell you the truth, I'm relieved" (p. 125). But concession is not comprehension, and Guildenstern, baffled even at the moment of death, asks:

> But why? Was it all for this? Who are we that so much should converge on our little deaths? (*In anguish to the Player:*) who are we? (p. 122)

And the Player replies, "You are Rosencrantz and Guildenstern. That's enough" (p. 122). That there is no other life for Rosencrantz and Guildenstern outside of the Shakespeare play, outside of their roles, is affirmed by Stoppard's final tableau, in which the bodies of Rosencrantz and Guildenstern become the subject of the ceremony afforded Hamlet in Olivier's film version, receiving all the circumstance due dead heroes. For Rosencrantz and Guildenstern are indeed heroes, having fulfilled (though less than nobly) their obligation in life and in the play, which is to perform.

What Rosencrantz and Guildenstern never realize is that they are part of a larger action than that of their own little lives. The two may go to their deaths without resistance, but they never comprehend what it means to be part of a greater plan. From his limited perspective, Guildenstern blames their fate on the boat:

> Where we went wrong was getting on a boat. We can move, of course, change direction, rattle about, but our movement is contained within a larger one that carries us along as inexorably as the wind and the current. . . . (p. 122)

Though he doesn't know it, Guildenstern's boat has metaphorical import, offering a wry comment on modern man's faith in free will and a bold statement on the nature of art. The confinement of which Guildenstern speaks suggests the limitations of both the individual in life and the character in drama, both of whom are free, "within limits, of course" (p. 116). The inexorability describes the demands imposed both upon man by virtue of the inevitability of death and upon the dramatic character by virtue of the script. Indeed, the preoccupation with death is quite obvious in the play, in which Guildenstern observes the "curious scientific phenomenon . . . that the fingernails grow after death, as does the beard" (p. 18); in which Rosencrantz wonders whether Guildenstern ever thinks of himself as "actually *dead*, lying in a box with a lid on it" (p. 70); and in which Rosencrantz asks:

> Whatever became of the moment when one first knew about death? There must have been one, a moment, in childhood when it first occurred to you that you don't go on for ever. (pp. 71–72)

The irony of their intellectual speculations is that they are just that, reflecting neither furstration nor perspicacity, and never acknowledging that Rosencrantz and Guildenstern are themselves not far from annihilation. Even more ironic is their failure to realize that each footstep into the arena of the *Hamlet* action, however tentative and however necessary, is another submission to the destiny of the script, which prescribes both their reason for being and their certain demise.

In their confusion and fear, Rosencrantz and Guildenstern never suspect that they may fare better as fictional characters than as real ones, for once they enter the *Hamlet* play they become part of an ordered universe which could not permit a coin to turn up heads ninety-two times. As the head of the players explains, ". . . there's a design at work in all art. . . . Events must play themselves out to aesthetic, moral and logical conclusion" (p. 79). Furthermore, in the world of play, the dead actor can rise again for an encore. As preoccupied with *ars moriendi* as Rosencrantz and Guildenstern are with the fact of death, the Player boasts that "it's what the actors do best. . . . They can die heroically, comically, ironically, slowly, suddenly, disgustingly,

charmingly, or from a great height . . . [and] they kill beau-
tifully" (p. 83). Not so committed to art as the Player, Guildenstern disparages such death, calling it cheap and unconvincing.
Yet the Player tells the story of a real onstage death that simply
didn't persuade the audience of its reality. And he later proves
that Guildenstern's defense of real death is empty, for Guildenstern cannot tell the difference between reality and illusion
when he stabs the Player. Apparently mortally wounded, the
Player falls to the floor and expires, only to be applauded by his
cohorts as he rises again.

The subjects of role and art are frequent ones in Stoppard's
writing, and much of what he offers here anticipates the philosophy and technique of The Real Inspector Hound. In Rosencrantz
and Guildenstern Are Dead, however, the play-within-a-play
structure produces a somewhat different effect. In The Real Inspector Hound Stoppard toys with the concept of the mimetic
quality of art, creating situations in the frame play and the inner
play which are strikingly similar. In Rosencrantz and Guildenstern Are Dead, mimesis, like the ill-fated pair, is dead. The
dumb show may preserve its sanctity, but the inner play proper
neither reflects nor distorts the reality of the outer play, for Rosencrantz and Guildenstern prove to have no existence outside
Hamlet. Their entire time in the outer play is overshadowed by
our knowledge that they are Shakespeare's, and not Stoppard's,
characters; like modern man alienated from an orderly world,
their "real" lives only serve to anticipate their immortal roles.
Where in The Real Inspector Hound the Muldoon Manor play
succeeds in encompassing the outer play, in Rosencrantz and
Guildenstern Are Dead, Hamlet absorbs its frame completely,
rendering the protagonists without their Hamlet roles nonenti-
ties. In both plays, whether the characters' fates are determined
by the slick whodunit play or the Shakespearean masterpiece,
the power of Stoppard's art is supreme.

ॐ Seven

Metafictional Theater: Handke's
The Ride Across Lake Constance

THE THEATER OF Peter Handke is by far the most self-conscious of all the playwrights studied here, not simply in terms of self-referentiality, but in its overall assertion of theater as a self-sufficient entity. In its persistent characterization of itself as something apart from the elements of reality, dependent upon no external references, the theater of Peter Handke is the culmination of the modern dramatist's concern with his own art. Richard Gilman has appropriately applied to Handke the remark which Beckett is said to have made of Joyce: "he is not writing about something, he is writing something." [1]

The challenge of finding a form of pure fiction has been articulated in the theoretical writings of Gustave Flaubert, Virginia Woolf, and Oscar Wilde,[2] among many others. And it has perhaps never been implemented more successfully than in Beckett's *The Lost Ones*. As Raymond Federman points out, that short novel attempts to be "the perfect voiceless fiction, which sets out to free itself of all connections with creator, narrator, voice, teller. . . ." It "establishes its own rules of order and chaos" and presents a form which, relieved of its mimetic function, is "free to create new meanings."[3] One would think that in drama the fact of physical presence would make the challenge of creating a self-sufficient world even more difficult, but Handke has succeeded in creating just such an illusion in *The Ride Across Lake Constance*.

In an essay entitled "The Film and the Theatre: The Misery of Comparison," Handke points to the nearly automatic need we have to compare:

> . . . I see, outside in the street, two streetsweepers cleaning the sidewalk with huge brooms. Both have orange and white striped uniforms *like bicycle racers*, both have white, crumpled stockings *like tramps* or *like characters in a Beckett play*, both have faces *like Southerners*, both wear caps *like those in photographs of prisoners of war from the First World War*, both walk stiffed-kneed *like bums*, all three—now a third joins them, and a fourth—wear black mittens *like the snow removal crew in the winter*, all five are alike with their gigantic brooms and shovels, which make them appear quite small, *like figures in a painting by Breughel*.
> But—one of the streetsweepers swept *faster than* the other, and the other streetsweeper wore his cap *lower* on his face *than* the one, and the other other streetsweeper had a much *more German* face *than* the other streetsweeper, and the other other streetsweeper seemed to perform his work *more unwillingly than* the other other streetsweeper, and finally—meanwhile the men have moved from my view—the last streetsweeper came to mind because he had, it seemed, shoved the broom forward *more powerfully than* the others.[4]

For centuries the drama has been *like* life; indeed, its main task has been to represent life. But Handke feels there should be no apparent mimetic relationship between the two; drama should be pure fiction, which does not depend for its understanding on any comparison to the real world. It should be "intense[ly] artificial," "endlessly *unusual*, unfamiliar," with the result that

> An unheard-of simultaneity of sight, breath, and discrimination is created. The space forms a theatrical unity, in which one becomes increasingly self-conscious and tense, almost to the point that the socially protective adhesive tape with which everyone wraps himself is ripped, is no longer visible, not only without, but also within, in the consciousness of the viewer.[5]

In Handke's theater, nothing is intended to be representational. Props, language, action, and actors correspond only tangentially to the usual patterns and characteristics of reality, with each attempting to signify nothing but itself. The event on stage exists on stage and claims only to be a theatrical event. Following a production in Paris of the Bread and Puppet Theatre from New York, Handke spoke of his conviction that direct presentation of actions and words should replace the traditional dramaturgy, which uses only those actions and words which serve the story. Handke hopes to create a theater in which actions and words

> become incidents which show nothing else, but present themselves as theatrical events. Actions act themselves and words talk themselves. The viewer, who awaits in the theatre the resolution of every word and every action, the thematic sense, the story, will be left with the action alone. The raising of a hand is a story. Buzzing is a story. Sitting, lying, and standing are stories. A very exciting story is the striking of a hammer against iron. Every word, every sound, every movement is a story: they lead to nothing, they remain visible for themselves alone. Every utterance is *made*; no action results naturally from the preceding action; no utterance means anything other than itself—it signifies itself.[6]

In 1966, Handke, then only twenty-four, stood before a Group 47 meeting in Princeton and disparaged the writings of the older members of this postwar association of German intellectuals for placing too much emphasis on description:

> He railed against . . . impotent narrative; empty stretches of descriptive (instead of analytic) writing . . . ; monotonous verbal litanies, regional and native idyllicism, which lacked spirit and creativeness.[7]

Yet to say that Handke's drama—or Beckett's, for that matter—has no relationship whatsoever to reality would be to affirm an impossibility. For Handke's drama, even in its disavowal of that relationship, ultimately says a good deal about reality. As Stanley Kauffmann says of Handke's plays, "the *whole* is all."[8] Despite the individual insignificance of every aspect of the theatrical event in mimetic terms, the "whole" of a Handke play is metaphor, which may finally be the way in which the art of the future finds justification.

Possibly the greatest influence (whether direct or indirect) on the philosophy of Handke is his fellow-Austrian Ludwig

Wittgenstein. That twentieth-century philosopher holds the distinction of being the only philosopher of repute who has developed two original philosophical systems, the second of which both expands upon and refutes the first. In both the earlier *Tractatus* (1920) and the posthumously published *Philosophical Investigations* (1951), Wittgenstein supports a linguistic investigation of reality, suggesting that all philosophical problems are created by linguistic confusion.[9]

In the *Tractatus*, Wittgenstein posits a "picture theory" which holds that there is a direct correlation between the arrangement of words into a sentence or proposition (*der Satz*) and the elements of the reality that sentence or proposition represents. Just as reality is the totality of facts, so language is the totality of propositions. And the words of those propositions relate to one another in the same way in which objects are related in reality. All "pictures," then, are models of reality and share the same form as reality, making language limited in being able to represent all possible situations but not the form itself. In the later *Philosophical Investigations*, Wittgenstein rejects the theory of a common logical form, thus freeing language from the limitations he had earlier suggested were imposed upon it by its very nature.

Like Wittgenstein, Handke is fascinated with the possibilities and the powers of language. The dialogue of *The Ride Across Lake Constance* (1971)—which Handke considers the culmination of his dramatic career to date—leaves the reader totally disoriented, unable to recognize a logical pattern in the language or any correlation between the language and events which are taking place or objects which are being named.[10] Yet *The Ride Across Lake Constance* emerges as a powerful comment on the nature of reality. Through bold and unconventional use of language, Handke accomplishes an annihilation of the predetermined structure of the theater and of reality itself, and suggests as well the possibility of a dramatic character which is not dependent upon a logical sequence of events for its identity and a real-life individual with an identity apart from that imposed upon him.

The set of *The Ride Across Lake Constance* is arranged in a manner which evokes instant recognition for the theater audience; the furnishings are those typical of the nineteenth-century drawing room, characteristically arranged. The stage directions read:

> All objects are in such a position that it would be difficult to imagine them standing elsewhere; it is as though they could not bear being moved ever so slightly. Everything appears as though rooted to the spot, not only the objects themselves but also the distances and empty spaces between them.[11]

Within moments of the play's opening, however, it is clear that the carefully arranged furniture is not before us because Handke wishes to create an impression of realism, but rather because he wants to undercut that impression, for in the context of Handke's unrealistic drama, the realistic drawing room quickly becomes precisely what it is: an obviously artificial stage set.

Emil Jannings and Heinrich George begin the play with a conversation more accurately called a linguistic game than communication.[12] What would constitute the exposition in traditional dramaturgy becomes an introduction to the language games that will be played and the questions regarding the relationship between reality and illusion that will be raised. Indeed, the first scene ends with George's declaration that "life is a game" (p. 87), a comment intended not as an epiphany but as a reference to just another clichéd expression which has lost its meaning (like "born loser," "born trouble-maker," "born criminal") and, by implication, to the relationship of the theater to reality, which has also become stale from habit. Earlier in their exchange Jannings had pointed to the blue sky on a cigar box label and proclaimed with profundity, "that blue sky you see on the label, my dear fellow, it really exists there" (p. 74). The sky is not a representation, just as the play is not a representation; both possess an autonomous reality. Jannings and George discuss an incident of the past, now reduced to a story, and question its present reality (pp. 75–76). And they name things, considering what each name designates and finding it ridiculous to speak of kidneys flambé, something that is not present, but quite satisfactory to talk of Jannings' rings, which have physical presence and correspond to and confirm the mental image of them (pp. 80–81). Jannings and George look around the room and pronounce names: "car," "cattle prod," "bloodhounds," "swollen bellies," "trigger button" (p. 81). But, of course, these names bear no relationship to what is on stage.

What, then, constitutes reality? Are the rings which are present in the phenomenal world and which can be identified by language the only reality? Or are the kidneys flambé, which can be recalled and named but are not now visible real? And what of objects that have physical presence but are either referred to by names which traditionally designate certain objects now without physical presence, or those which do not have the equivalent in an acceptable language pattern (such as "fiery Eskimos")? Are these reality? Is the world the totality of things, or is it, as Wittgenstein's *Tractatus* suggests, the totality of facts, or is it the totality of possibilities? And what then are the responsibilities and the limitations of language?

Language in the play is made up of nonsequiturs, examinations of the logical possibilities of a premise, alogical progressions, and confusions with respect to the designations of language, all designed to disturb our comfortable sense of the relationship of language and action to reality.

In one instance (p. 90), we see how language can be prescriptive. As Porten descends the stairs, George and Jannings count: "One, two, three, four, five, and seven!" When she hears "seven," she is just about to place her foot on the sixth step, becomes greatly disturbed, and retreats to the top of the stairs. She resumes her descent. "One, two, three, four, five, six, and seven!" But there is an eighth step, over which Porten stumbles; she is again upset, and rushes back to the top. On her third descent, she is accompanied by von Stroheim: "One, two, three, four, five, six, seven, eight, nine!" But there are only eight steps, and at the count of nine, they bounce on the floor, their knees buckle, and they stagger. It is a fine example of the lesson taught by the Einsager in Handke's earlier play, *Kaspar*: "If you see the object differently from the way you speak it, you must be mistaken." [13]

Jannings and George engage in a game of commands (pp. 93–95), each in turn demanding an object: "The boots!" "The newspaper!" "My glasses!" "The mustard!" "The hairbrush!" "The photo album!" "The pincers!" "The scalpel!" "The scissors!" "The pliers!" "The monkey wrench!" "The soldering iron!" "Hand over all your money!" "The sun!" When questioned "Why the sun?" Jannings defends his command: "Those are *my words*. I don't know why." And George insists, "Your saying so doesn't change anything." He has suggested the other side of the coin: where Porten's descent suggested the power of language to control reality, we now have the suggestion of a reality that exists independent of language, which may be designated by, but not altered by, language. Von Stroheim strongly objects: "Wrong! Entirely wrong!"

Other examples of the relationship or nonrelationship of language to reality occur. Porten asks, "What snowstorms?" long after snowstorms are mentioned (p. 92). George asks for the first time: "Once more: I offer you my fauteuil. . . . May I offer you my fauteuil?" (p. 91). Bergner cries, "Watch out! the candlestick is falling!" The candlestick remains motionless on the table (p. 92).

Von Stroheim and Porten tell stories of their awareness of the relationship between language and reality. Each has experienced an epiphany, an instance in which each, for a moment, fully understood language as a correlative of reality. Von Stroheim tells his story:

> I was sitting by a lakeshore in the morning and the lake was sparkling. Suddenly I noticed: the lake is *sparkling*. It is really sparkling. (p. 114)

And Porten tells hers:

> Something similar happened to me one time when someone told me that his pockets were empty. "My pockets are empty!" I didn't believe him and he turned his pockets inside out. They really were empty. Incredible! (p. 114)

The action sequences in *The Ride Across Lake Constance* do not conform to any recognizably real action; they consist of unmotivated acts and alogical responses, yet the pattern these actions form appears familiar. Jannings and George, for example, form in a series of gestures which are observed by Bergner, apparently without judgment: the two slap each other's thighs, pull each other's ears, and pat each other's cheeks; then Jannings shows George the back of his hand, George makes a circle with his forefinger and thumb and holds his hand in front of his face; Jannings holds his hands above his head, clasping one hand with the thumb and forefinger of the other hand and letting the clasped hand circle about (p. 88). Each gesture bears no apparent causal relationship to the next, but the series is smoothly enacted and is followed by an outburst of laughter by the two men and exclamations of "Exactly!" "You guessed it!" There has apparently been some form of communication, some understanding involved in the silent actions, but it is one that is alien to the audience's preconceived notions of logically motivated and interpreted action.

In another sequence involving von Stroheim and Porten, gestures which begin as apparent signs of affection end in apparent violence, and the final act is palpably alogical. Von Stroheim first places his finger under Porten's chin, lifting her face, then strokes the back of her head and pats her fondly on the shoulder. These actions are followed by his drumming two fingers on her cheek, snapping his fingers against her teeth, lowering her eyelid with his finger, and patting her rather hard on the buttocks. The sequence culminates in Porten's being positioned with her back to von Stroheim, Jannings kicking George, and Porten tumbling across the stage as though it were she who had been kicked, leaving von Stroheim standing with the left knee raised, ready to kick her (pp. 96–97).

Not all action sequences are ones which, in not conforming to our traditional patterns, appear absurd. Some are actions which have usual associations but here are stripped bare, revealing simple, dissociated actions:

PORTEN: Someone keeps looking over his shoulder while he's walking. Does he have a guilty conscience?
BERGNER: No, he simply looks over his shoulder from time to time.
PORTEN: Someone is sitting there with lowered head. Is he sad?
BERGNER: No, he simply sits there with lowered head.
PORTEN: Someone is flinching. Conscience-stricken?
BERGNER: No, he's simply flinching.
PORTEN: Two people sit there, don't look at each other, and are silent. Are they angry with one another?
BERGNER: No, they simply sit there, don't look at each other, and are silent!
PORTEN: Someone bangs on the table. To get his way?
BERGNER: Couldn't he for once simply bang on the table?

(pp. 107–8)

In Handke's theater, every act and every word finds significance in itself; it does not represent. In traditional drama and in life, no action or word is free from the previous one and no action or word exists for its own sake, for in traditional drama, as in life, action and language are arranged in patterns which have set interpretations. To Handke, language and action have become clichés, binding rather than liberating the thought which translates them. In his drama, language and action still constitute the play and they still fall into patterns, but the patterns are not the recognizable or expected ones. They are fresh combinations which have been freed to create new meanings. The Ride Across Lake Constance rejects clichés, presenting instead that "intensely artificial and endlessly unusual" event of which Handke speaks, and creating a self-conscious theater which exists not mimetically but as its own spontaneous reality.

If the world of Handke's play has equal status with reality, what then happens to the dichotomy which we have been discussing as existing in the fictive character? In each of the plays studied here, it was characteristic of the playwright to establish the existence of two distinct but interrelated worlds, one of fiction and one of reality. Almost invariably these worlds eventually fused, dramatizing the overlapping relationship. The characters who populated these plays were frequently metaphors for the dichotomy of the real and the fictive, and in all cases embodied a duality which, when exploited, enabled their creators to examine illusion and reality.

Handke is obviously as aware as any of his predecessors of the inherent duality of the dramatic character. Because of his special theatrical intent, however, Handke's exploitation of this awareness takes the form not of emphasizing the duality but of eliminating it. The *dramatis personae* of *The Ride Across Lake Constance* are the epitome of the metafictional character, for they are actors, and nothing more: "the actors are and play themselves at one and the same time" (stage direction, p. 69). In an effort to negate any dual identity, Handke refuses to give them even fictive names. In the German text, the names of famous actors (Jannings, George, Bergner, von Stroheim, Porten, Kessler) are used, simply to avoid designations of Actor A and Actor B. But in performance, all of the actors are called by their own names. The result is that there is none of the usual consciousness on the part of an audience of an actor's assuming the part of a character for the sake of performance. Here we are viewing an individual who at the outset possesses no prescribed role identity. We are actually witnessing character-in-the-making. As the play progresses, the actors

> discover who they are onstage in terms of each other, give each
> other identities, play identities, are captured by their identities—
> their identities become their roles or vice versa; are held together
> by the relationships they establish with each other—which at first
> are only a playing, but into which they get locked.[14]

This singularity of character is part of Handke's direct presentation of the stage as a separate reality; the audience is not responding to the distinction between fiction and reality, even with respect to the actor himself.

At the core of Handke's examination is the question of the integrity of the concept of character in both drama and life. Traditionally, as discussed in the introduction to this study, character in drama is formed primarily through action, including, of course, verbal action. So long as that action remains original, there is the possibility of original character. Once it becomes locked into patterns, however, the possibility ceases, and what is produced is the kind of interchangeable personality Ionesco dramatizes in *The Bald Soprano* and Handke suggests through the entrance of the identical Kessler twins at the end of *The Ride Across Lake Constance*. Handke's drama, through the destruction of pattern, attempts to renew the possibility of character both in drama and in life.

An earlier play by Handke, *Kaspar* (1968), confirms the playwright's concern with the creation of character. In that play he approaches the problem through an autistic man who at the play's outset knows only one sentence: "I want to be a person like somebody else was once." That sentence is Kaspar's only contact with reality and claim to identity. Whatever his observation, whatever his action, he gives meaning to it by reciting the one sentence which is uniquely his. It is not long, however, before the *Einsager* [15] begin the education of Kaspar. These disembodied voices teach Kaspar speech: he learns to clarify objects with sentences, compare perceptions with sentences, and name things. He finds:

> Everything I can name is no longer ominous; everything that is no longer ominous belongs to me; I am at ease with everything that belongs to me; everything I am at ease with strengthens my self-confidence.   (pp. 88–89)

Most importantly, Kaspar learns that with language he can control reality:

> You can impose order on everything that appears chaotic: you can declare it ordered: every object can be what you designate it to be: if you *see* the object differently from the way you *speak* of it, you must be mistaken: you must say to yourself, then it is obvious that you want to be *forced*, and thus do want to say it in the end.
> (p. 102)

It is the very a priori order of language, though, that Handke is rebelling against. When Kaspar knows only one sentence, a sentence which bears no relation to external reality but which represents his own unique reality, he is an individual. When he learns model sentences, however, and can apply them to reality, making his conception of reality fit those sentences, then he becomes simply another mass-produced nonindividual. Another Kaspar, in fact, physically joins Kaspar I on stage and is followed by several others, all computer print-outs of Kaspar I. When Kaspar first begins learning language, he is able to say "I am who I am." When his education is complete, he can only say, "I am who I am only accidentally." [16] Kaspar is locked into language, dependent for a definition of himself upon an imposed linguistic system which precludes creativity of thought and the consequent uniqueness of the individual. The result for Kaspar is existential despair.

Handke is obviously aware of the stagnation of the creation of character not only in drama but in life. His plays dramatize the fact that identity is no longer an individual's essence, but the product of prescribed responses. In *The Ride Across Lake Constance*, because Bergner has been tender previously, she is expected to be tender now; her past action has committed her present action. Von Stroheim and George demonstrate how one of them can identify a person on the strength of predetermined associations:

VON STROHEIM: . . . someone fondles an object or leans against it?
GEORGE: The proprietor.
VON STROHEIM: Someone moves with hunched shoulders among objects, makes a curve around them?
GEORGE: The guest.
VON STROHEIM: Someone who is squinting holds an object in his hand?
GEORGE: The thief.   (p. 116)

Von Stroheim abhors how readily actions are translated into patterned meanings. He insists it is as ridiculous to interpret someone's feelings or thoughts by his actions as it is to call an easy chair a life preserver (p. 117). And he demonstrates how he can predict responses: by asking Jannings what he has in his mouth he can make Jannings remove his cigar; by asking Jannings why his collar button is open he can make Jannings close his collar button; by drawing attention to Jannings' seriousness he can make Jannings laugh (p. 118). For Handke, character in life has become the fixed entity it has been in drama. Not only do we learn to interpret a person's character by his actions, we also learn to expect certain actions of him. And, even more importantly, the person begins to respond in accordance with our expectations. Bergner asks:

> Do I talk too much for you? Are my knees too bony? Am I too heavy for you? Is my nose too big? Am I too sensible for you? Do you find me too loud? Are my breasts too small? Do you think I'm too fat? Am I too fast for you? Am I too skinny for you? Was I good? (p. 124)

And Jannings assesses her remarks: "You see, she herself uses the categories in which one thinks of her" (p. 124). When this line of characterization is carried to the extreme, the terrifying result is an unthinking automaton, completely submissive to control, which Jannings describes:

> They did it once without my saying anything while they were half asleep, or because it just happened like that. Then I said it and they did it again. Then they asked me: "May I do that for you?" and I said: "You shall!" And from then on they did it without my having to say anything. It had become the custom. I could point my *foot* at something and they would jump and get it. . . . An order resulted; and for people to continue to socialize with one another, this order was made explicit; it was formulated. And once it had been formulated, people had to stick to it because, after all, they had formulated it. (p. 122)

The characters in Handke's play operate in a kind of dream world, an anesthetized state of unawareness that automatically accepts the habits of life. No image is more common in *The Ride Across Lake Constance* than sleep: the play opens with Jannings seated in an armchair, his eyes closed; George enters and stumbles because his foot has fallen asleep, and Jannings admits that his hand has also. Throughout the play various characters fall asleep and Handke's remarks direct that a particular character respond as though he were asleep. And the question "Are You Dreaming or Are You Speaking?" serves as the play's epigraph. The play is populated with semicomatose individuals no longer capable of seeing or hearing themselves. Their patterns of action and speech, though unfamiliar to us, are much the same as our own patterns, which have been deadened by habit and no longer stimulate thought. In Handke's theater, this somnambulistic state is exposed and assaulted until language, character, and the theater begin "to take on, like the color returning to the cheeks of a nearly hanged man, the signs of a strange and unexpected resurrection."[17] At the end of Handke's play the audience can exclaim with Bergner, "I saw myself! I noticed myself! I heard myself!" (p. 107).

The title of The Ride Across Lake Constance refers to "Der Reiter und der Bodensee," a poem by Gustav Schwab, which tells of a horseman who rode fearlessly across a frozen lake only to die when he reached the other side and was told how thin the ice he had traversed was. Nicholas Hern suggests that the thin ice is a metaphor for the state of somnambulism we and the characters of Handke's play are in and of which we must remain unaware if we are not finally to "disintegrate with shock."[18] And Botho Strauss points to the analogy between language and Handke's play:

> The ride parallels the functioning of our grammar, of our system of coordinating perception and meaning, and of our linguistic and sentient powers of reason; it is only a provisional, permeable order, which, particularly when, as in Handke's play, it becomes conscious of its own existence, is threatened by . . . schizophrenia and madness.[19]

But we may just as readily be jolted into a constructive awareness as into death when we recognize the fragility of the relationship between language and reality, and it is this kind of awareness that Handke is trying to achieve. He is trying to revitalize language, revitalize the signs of reality, so that they reflect a meaningful relationship between external reality and an inner, individual reality.

Like the other playwrights who are the subject of this study, Handke dramatizes the need of modern man to redefine and re-create the relationship between reality and illusion in both a philosophical and an artistic sense. Philosophically, the illusion of a solipsistic world which Handke's theater achieves is an explainable and predictable outgrowth of that need; artistically, it is the evolutionary extension of the self-referential theater of his predecessors.

After Pirandello, Genet, Beckett, Weiss, Albee, and Stoppard,

Handke's startlingly unconventional theater should not be unexpected. Pirandello's tentative questionings of the right of art to be separately defined, Genet's blatant assertion of the superiority of illusion, Beckett's unimpassioned observation of man's need for the illusion of meaning, Weiss's kaleidoscopic perspectives of the individual and of history, Albee's qualified denial of alternate realities (excepting art), and Stoppard's playful fusion of the fictive and the real—all reflect the modern artist's ongoing awareness of the constantly changing dialectic of reality and illusion. It is this dialectic which Handke dramatizes, not by emphasizing the dichotomy, but by seeming to eliminate it.

In creating a self-consciously self-sufficient world, Handke, among the most innovative of contemporary dramatists, goes beyond the illusion of reality. And in appearing to eliminate the dichotomy between the real and the fictive with respect to his characters, in creating purely metafictional characters, he succeeds in annihilating the mimetic function of art. Some half a century after Pirandello began the "other tradition" in modern drama, Handke, in *The Ride Across Lake Constance*, demonstrates its continuing significance by emphatically asserting the autonomy of both illusion and art.

✎Notes

Introduction

1. John Simon, *Uneasy Stages: A Chronicle of the New York Theater, 1963–1973* (New York: Random House, 1975), pp. 366–67.

2. F. R. Leavis, *The Great Tradition* (Garden City, N.Y.: Doubleday, 1954).

3. Alter, *Partial Magic*, p. xii.

4. For a survey of self-consciousness in literature through Shakespeare, see Anne Righter, *Shakespeare and the Idea of the Play*. For a discussion of the phenomenon in Shakespeare's plays, see James L. Calderwood, *Shakespearean Metadrama*, and Robert Egan, *Drama Within Drama*. Ruby Cohn recaps and continues Righter's survey into modern dramatic literature in "The Role and the Real," in *Currents in Contemporary Drama*, pp. 198–257.

5. Bernard Shaw, *Fanny's First Play*, in *Complete Plays with Prefaces*, 6 vols. (New York: Dodd, Mead, 1962), 6:261.

6. Alter, *Partial Magic*, p. x.

7. Alain Robbe-Grillet, "From Realism to Reality," in *For a New Novel: Essays on Fiction*, Richard Howard, trans. (New York: Grove Press, 1965), p. 158. First published by Les Éditions de Minuit, Paris, as *Pour un nouveau roman*, 1963.

8. Alter, *Partial Magic*, p. 220.

9. Irving Howe, ed., *The Idea of the Modern in Literature and the Arts* (New York: Horizon Press, 1967), pp. 14–15.

10. R. D. Laing, *The Politics of Experience* (New York: Ballantine Books, 1971), p. 43. Reprint of Pantheon Books edition, 1967.

11. Howe, *The Idea of the Modern in Literature and the Arts*, p. 17.

12. Howe, p. 17.

13. Joe David Bellamy, ed., *Super Fiction*, p. 5.

14. Elizabeth Burns, *Theatricality*, p. 31.

15. Robert W. Corrigan, "The Disavowal of Identity in the Modern Theatre," in *The Theatre in Search of a Fix* (New York: Dell, 1974), pp. 202–9. Reprint of Delacorte Press edition, 1973; essay originally appeared, in different form, in Robert W. Corrigan, ed., *The New Theatre of Europe*, vol. 2 (New York: Dell, 1964).

16. Hubert C. Heffner, "Pirandello and the Nature of Man." Heffner's hierar-

121

chy of differentiation, in ascending order of importance, is: biological; physical; bent or disposition; traits of feeling, emotion, passion; deliberation, expedient or ethical; and decision. Heffner is careful to point out that the choice which is the highest level of characterization may eventuate in either words or physical deeds: "Frequently only that eventuation in physical deeds is called action; but this is wrong. In drama any exercise of the will, however it eventuates, is action" (p. 260).

17. Francis Fergusson, The Idea of a Theater: The Art of Drama in Changing Perspective (Garden City, N.Y.: Doubleday, n.d.), pp. 24–25. Reprint of Princeton University Press edition, 1949.

18. Heffner, "Pirandello and the Nature of Man," pp. 263–64.

19. Heffner, p. 264.

20. Joseph Wood Krutch, "Pirandello and the Dissrlution of the Ego," pp. 65–87.

21. Heffner, "Pirandello and the Nature of Man," pp. 255–56.

22. Tom Stoppard, Rosencrantz and Guildenstern Are Dead (New York: Grove Press, 1967), p. 39.

23. Edmund Fuller, Man in Modern Fiction: Some Minority Opinions on Contemporary American Writing (New York: Random House, 1958), p. 12.

24. Robert W. Corrigan, "The Transformation of the Individual in the Modern Theatre," in The Theatre in Search of a Fix, p. 195. Essay originally appeared, in different form, in Robert W. Corrigan, ed., The New Theatre of Europe, vol. 1 (New York: Dell, 1962).

25. Charles Child Walcutt, Man's Changing Mask: Modes and Methods of Characterization in Fiction (Minneapolis: University of Minnesota Press, 1966), p. 6.

26. Krutch, "Pirandello and the Dissolution of the Ego," pp. 77–79.

27. Jean Genet, Our Lady of the Flowers, Bernard Frechtman, trans. (New York: Bantam Books, 1964), p. 221. Reprint of Grove Press edition, 1963. First published by L'Arbalète of Lyons, France, as Notre-Dame des Fleurs, 1943; revised version published by Gallimard, Paris, 1951.

28. Claire Rosenfield, "The Shadow Within: The Conscious and Unconscious Use of the Double," in Albert J. Guerard, ed., Stories of the Double (Philadelphia: Lippincott, 1967), p. 331. First published in Daedalus (Spring 1963), 92:326–44.

29. Michel de Ghelderode, The Death of Doctor Faust, in George Hauger, ed., Seven Plays, 2 vols. (New York: Hill & Wang, 1964), 2:147. First published by Gallimard, Paris, 1950.

30. Ghelderode, from The Ostend Interviews, in Hauger, Seven Plays, 1:96.

31. Ghelderode, The Death of Doctor Faust, pp. 140–41.

1: Pirandello's Henry IV

1. Francis Fergusson, The Idea of a Theater: The Art of Drama in Changing Perspective (Garden City, N.Y.: Doubleday, n.d.), p. 206.

2. Ironically, Pirandello did not enjoy instant popularity in Italy. The 1921 production of Six Characters in Rome resulted in a chaotic show of displeasure

from which Pirandello and his daughter Lietta narrowly escaped. Pirandello is known to have sulked over his reputation in his native country, at one point remarking that Italy would "have to live down the shame of having misunderstood." When *Lazarus* was unkindly received in 1929 (though mainly on religious grounds), he decided to take his next play, *Tonight We Improvise*, to Germany, saying, "I have become a stranger to my own country and . . . I shall therefore have to win another home for my art." Quotations are taken from Robert Brustein, *The Theatre of Revolt*, pp. 282–83.

3. Henri Beraud, *Retours à pied* (Paris: G. Crès, 1925), pp. 178–79; Pierre Brisson, *Au Hasard des soirées* (Paris: Gallimard, 1935), p. 317. Quoted in Thomas Bishop, *Pirandello and the French Theater*, p. 147.

4. Statement by Georges Neveux in "Pirandello vous a-t-il influencé?" *Arts* (January 16, 1957), no. 602; quoted in Bishop, *Pirandello and the French Theater*, p. 147.

5. Alfred Mortier, *Quinze ans de théâtre* (Paris: Albert Messein, 1933), p. 279; quoted in Bishop, p. 7.

6. Gaston Rageot, "Le Pirandellisme," *Revue politique et littéraire* (June 19, 1926), 64(12):383; quoted in Bishop, p. 8.

7. Marcel Doisy, *Le Théâtre français contemporain* (Brussels: La Boétie, 1947), p. 272; quoted in Bishop, p. 9.

8. Brustein, *The Theatre of Revolt*, p. 282.

9. Brustein, p. 296.

10. Luigi Pirandello, *Six Characters in Search of an Author*, Edward Storer, trans., in Eric Bentley, ed., *Naked Masks: Five Plays by Luigi Pirandello* (New York: E. P. Dutton, 1957), p. 264. Pirandello's plays are available in the original Italian in *Maschere Nude*, 2 vols. (Milan: Arnoldo Mondadori, 1958).

11. Pirandello, *Six Characters in Search of an Author*, p. 265.

12. Luigi Pirandello, *Henry IV*, Edward Storer, trans., in Bentley, ed., *Naked Masks*, p. 159; subsequent page references will appear parenthetically in the text.

13. Oscar Wilde, "The Decay of Lying" (1889), in Richard Ellmann, ed., *The Artist as Critic: Critical Writings of Oscar Wilde* (New York: Random House, 1969), pp. 290–91.

14. The first edition of *On Humor*, which was based on lectures given by Pirandello in Rome, appeared in 1908. The "second, enlarged edition" appeared in 1920. Quotations are from the second edition, excerpted and translated by Teresa Novel in *Tulane Drama Review* (Spring 1966), 10(3):46–59; quotations in text appear on p. 52.

15. Samuel Beckett, *Proust* (New York: Grove Press, 1957). First published by Chatto and Windus, 1931.

16. The play (p. 142) refers to January 25, 1071, as the date when Henry knelt before Canossa. The historical date, however, according to Eric Bentley, *Theatre of War: Comments on 32 Occasions* (New York: Viking Press, 1972), p. 35, was five years later.

17. The phrase is that of C. F. Keppler, who discusses the concept of the double in "The Picture of Dorian Gray" in *The Literature of the Second Self* (Tucson: University of Arizona Press, 1972), pp. 79–82.

18. Pirandello, *On Humor*, in TDR, p. 50.

19. Adriano Tilgher, "Life Versus Form," from *Studi sul teatro contempo-*

raneo (Rome: Libreria di Scienze e Lettere, 1923, 1928), Glauco Cambon, trans., in Glauco Cambon, ed., *Pirandello*, p. 21.
20. Tilgher, p. 21.
21. Brustein, *The Theatre of Revolt*, p. 286.
22. Pirandello, *On Humor*, in *TDR*, pp. 48, 50.
23. Tilgher, "Life Versus Form," p. 23.
24. Tilgher, p. 24.
25. Quoted by J. H. Whitfield, s.v. "Pirandello, Luigi," in *Encyclopaedia Britannica*, 1975 ed.

2: Genet's Maids, Brothel Patrons, and Blacks

1. Antonin Artaud, *The Theatre and Its Double*, Mary Caroline Richards, trans. (New York: Grove Press, 1958). First published by Gallimard, Paris, as *Le Théâtre et son Double*, in *Collection Métamorphoses*, no. 4, 1938. For a useful analysis of Artaud's theater, see Bettina L. Knapp, *Antonin Artraud: Man of Vision* (New York: Avon Books, 1969).
2. Artaud, p. 31.
3. Artaud, p. 48.
4. Susan Sontag, ed., introduction to *Antonin Artaud: Selected Writings*, Helen Weaver, trans. (New York: Farrar, Straus & Giroux, 1976), p. xxix.
5. Jean Genet, *The Thief's Journal*, Bernard Frechtman, trans. (New York: Bantam Books, 1965), pp. 157–58. Reprint of Grove Press edition, 1964; first published by Gallimard, Paris, as *Journal du Voleur*, 1949.
6. Jean Genet, *The Balcony*, rev. ed., Bernard Frechtman, trans. (New York: Grove Press, 1958), pp. 35, 36; subsequent page references will appear parenthetically in the text. The original version of *Le Balcon* was first published by Décines (*L'Arbalète*), Isère, France, in 1956; the Frechtman translation is based on the revised version, published by Barbezat in 1962.
7. Richard N. Coe, *The Vision of Jean Genet*, p. 213.
8. Coe, p. 214.
9. See page 13 of this study for quotation from Genet's *Our Lady of the Flowers*.
10. Sydney S. Walter, "The Maids Performed by Men," *The Village Voice*, October 29, 1964, rpt. in Richard N. Coe, ed., *The Theater of Jean Genet*, p. 60.
11. Jean-Paul Sartre, preface to Genet, *The Maids and Deathwatch*, p. 8.
12. Jean Genet, *The Maids*, in *The Maids and Deathwatch*, rev. ed., Bernard Frechtman, trans. (New York: Grove Press, 1961), p. 39; subsequent page references will appear parenthetically in the text. The original version of *Les Bonnes* was first published in *L'Arbalète* (May 1947), no. 12, pp. 47–92.
13. Sartre, preface to *The Maids*, p. 10.
14. From an anonymous interview in *L'Express* (April 26, 1957), no. 305, in Richard N. Coe, ed., *The Theater of Jean Genet*, p. 89.
15. For Genet's account of this incident, see Sartre, *Saint Genet*, p. 427.
16. From "Something for Everybody," *The Observer* (London), April 28, 1957, in Coe, *The Theater of Jean Genet*, pp. 87–88.
17. Sartre, preface to *The Maids*, p. 7.

18. Tom F. Driver, *Romantic Quest and Modern Query: History of the Modern Theater* (New York: Delacorte Press, 1970), p. 447.

19. Jean Genet, *The Blacks: A Clown Show*, Bernard Frechtman, trans. (New York: Grove Press, 1960); subsequent page references will appear parenthetically in the text. *Les Nègres* was first published by Décines (*L'Arbalète*), Isère, France, in 1958.

20. Ruby Cohn, *Currents in Contemporary Drama* (Bloomington: Indiana University Press, 1969), p. 242.

21. Sartre, preface to *The Maids*, p. 7.

22. Artaud, *The Theatre and Its Double*, p. 31.

23. Jean Genet, "A Note on Theatre" (foreword to 1954 edition of *The Maids*), in Morris Kelly, ed., *Genet/Ionesco*, p. 20.

3: Beckett's Didi and Gogo, Hamm and Clov

1. Katharine Worth, "The Space and Sound in Beckett's Theatre," in *Beckett the Shape Changer*, p. 185.

2. G. C. Barnard, *Samuel Beckett*, pp. 90–91.

3. Eugene Webb, *The Plays of Samuel Beckett*, p. 27.

4. John Fletcher and John Spurling, *Beckett*, pp. 59–60; they make specific reference to the line in which Vladimir refers to the area occupied by the audience as a bog and the incident in which Vladimir stops Estragon from running in *that* direction, i.e., toward the audience.

5. Samuel Beckett, *Waiting for Godot* (New York: Grove Press, 1954), p. 8; subsequent page references will appear parenthetically in the text. (Since this edition numbers only every other page, unnumbered pages are designated by the number of the facing page.) *En Attendant Godot* was firt published by Éditions de Minuit, Paris, in 1952.

6. Alain Robbe-Grillet, "Samuel Beckett, or 'Presence' in the Theatre," Barbara Bray, trans., in Martin Esslin, ed., *Samuel Beckett*, p. 108. First published by Les Éditions de Minuit, Paris, as *Pour un nouveau roman*, 1963.

7. Enoch Brater, "The 'Absurd' Actor in the Theatre of Samuel Beckett," p. 198.

8. Ruby Cohn, *Currents in Contemporary Drama* (Bloomington: Indiana University Press, 1969), p. 136.

9. Robbe-Grillet, "Samuel Beckett," p. 113.

10. This fact is recorded in Cohn, *Currents in Contemporary Drama*, p. 226. Beckett directed the production.

11. Samuel Beckett, *Endgame* (New York: Grove Press, 1958), p. 12; subsequent page references will appear parenthetically in the text. *Fin de partie* was first published by Éditions de Minuit, Paris, in 1957.

12. Worth, "The Space and Sound in Beckett's Theatre," pp. 186–87.

13. Ross Chambers, "An Approach to *Endgame*," in Bell Gale Chevigny, ed., *Endgame*, p. 78. First published as "Vers une interpretation de *Fin de partie*," *Studi Francesi* (gennaio-aprile 1967), no. 31, pp. 90–96.

14. Antony Easthope, "Hamm, Clov, and Dramatic Method in *Endgame*," in Chevigny, ed., p. 62. First published in *Modern Drama* (spring 1968),

10:424–33. Easthope's essay is an excellent one, and much of the discussion in the following paragraphs parallels his analysis.

15. Easthope, p. 65.

4: Weiss's Inmates at Charenton

1. Carl Enderstein, "The Symbiosis of the Arts and Peter Weiss's *Marat/Sade*," p. 3.

2. Sidney F. Parham, "*Marat/Sade*: The Politics of Experience, or the Experience of Politics?" p. 236.

3. Peter Weiss, *The Persecution and Assassination of Jean-Paul Marat As Performed by the Inmates of the Asylum of Charenton Under the Direction of the Marquis de Sade*, Geoffrey Skelton, trans. (New York: Atheneum, 1966), p. 99; subsequent page references will appear parenthetically in the text. *Die Verfolgung und Ermordung Jean Paul Marats, dargestellt durch die Schauspielgruppe des Hospizes zu Charenton unter Anleitung des Herrn de Sade* was first published by Suhrkamp Verlag, Frankfurt am Main, in 1964.

4. Quoted in Martin Esslin, *Reflections*, pp. 149–50.

5. Quoted in Esslin, p. 150.

6. Hans-Bernhard Moeller, "German Theater 1964," p. 164.

7. John Simon, in *Singularities: Essays on the Theater 1964–1974* (New York: Random House, 1975), p. 190, notes the mistranslation of *Gesichte* (visions) as *Gesichter* (faces).

8. Ruby Cohn, *Currents in Contemporary Drama* (Bloomington: Indiana University Press, 1969), p. 220.

9. Quoted in Ian Hilton, *Peter Weiss*, p. 46. The announcement was reprinted in *Neues Deutschland* and appears in *Theater Heute*, October 1965.

10. Third and fourth letters on language, dated, respectively, November 9, 1932 and May 28, 1933, in Antonin Artaud, *The Theater and Its Double*, Mary Caroline Richards, trans. (New York: Grove Press, 1958), pp. 115, 118; quoted in Susan Sontag, "Marat/Sade Artaud," p. 168.

11. Sontag, p. 169.

12. Richard Schechner, ed., "*Marat/Sade* Forum," pp. 215–16.

5: Albee's Martha and George

1. Joseph Wood Krutch, "Modernism" in *Modern Drama: A Definition and an Estimate* (Ithaca, N.Y.: Cornell University Press, 1953), p. 107.

2. C. W. E. Bigsby, *Confrontation and Commitment*, pp. 9–10.

3. Bigsby, p. 10.

4. Bigsby, p. 20.

5. John McCarten's review, "Long Night's Journey Into Daze," *The New Yorker*, October 20, 1962, may serve as an example of this sentiment: [The play is] "vulgar mishmash . . . it could be cut in half by the elimination of the 'goddamn's,' 'Jesus Christ's,' and other expressions designed, presumably, to show us that this is really modern stuff" (p. 85).

6. See, respectively, Robert Graham Kemper, "Allegory of the American Dream," pp. 1214–15; Forrest E. Hazard, "The Major Theme in *Who's Afraid of Virginia Woolf?*" pp. 10–11; Charlene M. Taylor, "Coming of Age in New Carthage: Albee's Grown-up Children," *Educational Theatre Journal* (March 1973), 25(1):52–65; Tom Driver, "What's the Matter with Edward Albee?"; Samuel Terrien, "Demons Also Believe," *The Christian Century* (December 9, 1970), 87(49):1481–86; Jean Gould, *Modern American Playwrights* (New York: Dodd, Mead, 1966), pp. 273–90.

7. Richard Schechner, "TDR Comment," *Tulane Drama Review* (Spring 1963), 7(3):8.

8. Richard E. Amacher, *Edward Albee*, p. 107.

9. Lawrence Kingsley, "Reality and Illusion: Continuity of a Theme in Albee," *Educational Theatre Journal* (March 1973), 25(1):72.

10. Edward Albee, *Who's Afraid of Virginia Woolf?* (New York: Atheneum, 1962), stage direction, p. 238; subsequent page references will appear parenthetically in the text.

11. This point was noticed by Max Halpern, "What Happens in Who's Afraid . . . ?" pp. 140–41.

12. Lionel Abel, *Metatheatre: A New View of Dramatic Form* (New York: Hill & Wang, 1963).

13. Josephine Waters Bennett, *Measure for Measure as Royal Entertainment* (New York: Columbia University Press, 1966).

14. Ruth Meyer, "Language," p. 65.

6: Stoppard's Moon and Birdboot, Rosencrantz and Guildenstern

1. Allardyce Nicoll, *English Drama: A Modern Viewpoint* (New York: Barnes & Noble, 1968).

2. John Russell Taylor, *The Angry Theatre: New British Drama* (rev. ed.; New York: Hill & Wang, 1969), p. 39. Earlier ed.: *Anger and After: A Guide to the New British Drama* (Baltimore: Penguin Books, 1962).

3. In support of this view, note Tom Stoppard's response to the interviewer's question of why he was writing drama, rather than novels or poetry, in "Ambushes for the Audience," p. 4: "Historical accident. After 1956 everybody of my age who wanted to write, wanted to write plays—after Osborne and the rest at the Court, and with Tynan on the Observer, and Peter Hall about to take over the RSC."

4. C. W. E. Bigsby, "Stoppard, Tom," in James Vinson, ed., *Contemporary Dramatists* (London: St. James Press; New York: St. Martin's Press, 1973), p. 737.

5. See William Babula, "The Play-Life Metaphor in Shakespeare and Stoppard," pp. 279–81.

6. Tom Stoppard, *The Real Inspector Hound* (New York: Grove Press, 1968), p. 10; subsequent page references will appear parenthetically in the text.

7. John Simon, *Uneasy Stages: A Chronicle of the New York Theater, 1963–1973* (New York: Random House, 1975), pp. 113–14.

8. Robert Brustein, "Waiting for Hamlet," p. 149.

9. Tom Stoppard, *Rosencrantz and Guildenstern Are Dead* (New York: Grove Press, 1967), p. 108; subsequent page references will appear parenthetically in the text.

7: Metafictional Theater: Handke's *The Ride Across Lake Constance*

1. Richard Gilman, *The Making of Modern Drama*, p. 277.

2. Gustave Flaubert, from Edmond and Jules de Goncourt, *Pages from the Goncourt Journal* [1861], Robert Baldick, ed. and trans. (London and New York, 1962), p. 58; letter to Louise Colet [1852], *Selected Letters*, Francis Steegmuller, trans. (London, 1954), pp. 127–28; Virginia Woolf, "Modern Fiction" [1919], from *The Common Reader* (I) (London and New York, 1925), pp. 184–95; Oscar Wilde, preface to *The Picture of Dorian Gray* [1891], *The Works of Oscar Wilde*, G. F. Maine, ed. (London, 1948), p. 17; all reprinted in Richard Ellmann and Charles Feidelson, Jr., eds., *The Modern Tradition: Backgrounds of Modern Literature* (New York: Oxford University Press, 1965), pp. 126, 126–27, 121–26, and 102–3, respectively.

3. Raymond Federman, "Samuel Beckett: The Cylinder of Fiction," paper presented at Modern Language Association Convention, San Francisco, 1975, p. 1.

4. Peter Handke, "Theatre and Film: The Misery of Comparison," Donald Nordberg, trans., in James Hurt, ed., *Focus on Film and Theatre* (Englewood Cliffs, N.J.: Prentice-Hall, 1974), p. 165. From *Prosa, Gedichte, Theaterstücke, Hörspiel, Aufsätze* (Frankfurt: Suhrkamp, 1969).

5. Handke, pp. 174–75.

6. Handke, p. 174.

7. Siegfried Mandel, *Group 47*, p. 193.

8. Stanley Kauffmann, *Persons of the Drama: Theater Criticism and Comment* (New York: Harper & Row, 1964), p. 195.

9. See Ludwig Wittgenstein, *Tractatus Logico-Philosophicus*, D. F. Pears and B. F. McGuinness, trans. (London: Routledge & Kegan Paul; New York: Humanities Press, 1961). First German edition in *Annalen der Naturphilosphie*, 1921. *Philosophical Investigations*, trans. G. E. M. Anscombe (New York: Macmillan Co., 1953).

10. Note, for example, Clive Barnes's remark following the Lincoln Center production of *The Ride Across Lake Constance*, published in "The Theatre: Peter Handke's *Ride Across Lake Constance*," *New York Times*, January 14, 1972, p. 16:

"To say I didn't understand Peter Handke's play "The Ride Across Lake Constance" . . . would be to underestimate shamefully the cavernous profundity of my ignorance. The play had only been going for two minutes when I realized that I did not know what was going on."

11. Peter Handke, *The Ride Across Lake Constance*, Michael Roloff, trans., in Michael Roloff, ed., *The Ride Across Lake Constance and Other Plays* (New York: Farrar, Straus & Giroux, 1976), p. 72; subsequent page references will ap-

pear parenthetically in the text. *Der Ritt über den Bodensee* was first published in *Theater Heute* (October 1970), vol. 11, no. 10, then by Suhrkamp Verlag, Frankfurt, in 1971.

12. As will be discussed later, for the sake of convenience, Handke uses names of well-known actors rather than designating the actors "Actor A," "Actor B," etc.

13. Peter Handke, *Kaspar*, Michael Roloff, trans., in Michael Roloff, ed., *Kaspar and Other Plays* (New York: Farrar, Straus & Giroux, 1969), p. 103; subsequent page references will appear parenthetically in the text. *Kaspar* was first published by Suhrkamp, Frankfurt, in 1967. The play also appears in *Theater Heute* (1968 Jahrbuch), *Spectaculum* (1969), vol. 12, and in Peter Handke, *Stücke 1* (Suhrkamp, 1972).

14. Michael Roloff, "Postscript: A Note on Methods," p. 165.

15. As Nicholas Hern points out in *Peter Handke, Einsager* is a "made-up word meaning 'in-sayers' but having something of the force of 'indoctrinators' or 'persuaders,' whose job it is to 'bring Kaspar to speech by speech' " (p. 62). Roloff translates the word "prompters," adding a theatrical connotation to the function of the *Einsager* as language guides.

16. This final line appears in the *Theater Heute* edition; it is altered in the 1972 edition and eliminated from the 1967 edition.

17. Gilman, *The Making of Modern Drama*, p. 271.

18. Hern, *Peter Handke*, p. 94.

19. Botho Strauss, "Versuch, äethetische und politische Ereignisse zusammenzudenken—Neues Theater 1967–70," *Theater Heute* 11, 10 (October 1970), 11(10):61–68; quoted (in translation) in Hern, p. 94.

℘Selected Bibliography of Criticism in English

Introduction

Abel, Lionel. Metatheatre: A New View of Dramatic Form. New York: Hill & Wang, 1963.

Alter, Robert. Partial Magic: The Novel as a Self-Conscious Genre. Berkeley: University of California Press, 1975.

Bellamy, Joe David, ed. Super Fiction or the American Story Transformed. New York: Vintage Books, 1975.

Bennett, Josephine Waters. Measure for Measure as Royal Entertainment. New York: Columbia University Press, 1966.

Burns, Elizabeth. Theatricality: A Study of Convention in the Theatre and in Social Life. New York: Harper & Row, 1973. First published by Longman Group, London, 1972.

Calderwood, James L. Shakespearean Metadrama: The Argument of the Play in Titus Andronicus, Love's Labour's Lost, Romeo and Juliet, A Midsummer Night's Dream, and Richard II. Minneapolis: University of Minnesota Press, 1971.

Caute, David. The Illusion: An Essay on Politics, Theatre and the Novel. New York: Harper & Row, 1971.

Cohn, Ruby. Currents in Contemporary Drama. Bloomington: Indiana University Press, 1969.

Egan, Robert. Drama Within Drama: Shakespeare's Sense of His Art in King Lear, The Winter's Tale, and The Tempest. New York: Columbia University Press, 1975.

Ehrmann, Jacques, ed. Game, Play, Literature. Boston: Beacon Press, 1968.

Epstein, Leslie. "Beyond the Baroque: The Role of the Audience in the Modern Theater." Tri-Quarterly (Spring 1968), 12:213–34.

Gassner, John. Directions in Modern Theatre and Drama: An Expanded Edition of Form and Idea in Modern Theatre, pp. 133–236. New York: Holt, Rinehart & Winston, 1965.

Goffmann, Erving. *The Presentation of Self in Everyday Life.* Garden City, N.Y.: Doubleday, 1959.

Grossvogel, David J. *20th Century French Drama.* New York: Columbia University Press, 1961. First published as *The Self-Conscious Stage in Modern French Drama,* 1958.

Heffner, Hubert C. "Pirandello and the Nature of Man." In Travis Bogard and William I. Oliver, eds., *Modern Drama: Essays in Criticism.* New York: Oxford University Press, 1965. Originally a lecture delivered at Carleton College, November 29, 1956. First published in *Tulane Drama Review* (June 1957), 1(3):23–40.

Huizinga, Johan. *Homo ludens: A Study of the Play-Element in Culture.* Boston: Beacon Press, 1950.

Nelson, Robert J. *Play within a Play: The Dramatist's Conception of His Art: Shakespeare to Anouilh.* New Haven: Yale University Press, 1958.

Righter, Anne. *Shakespeare and the Idea of the Play.* Baltimore: Penguin Books, 1967. First published by Chatto and Windus, London, 1962.

Pirandello

Bishop, Thomas. *Pirandello and the French Theater.* New York: New York University Press, 1960.

Brustein, Robert. *The Theatre of Revolt: Studies in Modern Drama from Ibsen to Genet,* pp. 279–318. Boston: Little, Brown, 1962.

Büdel, Oscar. *Pirandello.* New York: Hillary House, 1969.

Cambon, Glauco, ed. *Pirandello: A Collection of Critical Essays.* Englewood Cliffs, N.J.: Prentice-Hall, 1967.

Esslin, Martin. *Reflections: Essays on Modern Theatre,* pp. 47–56. Garden City, N.Y.: Doubleday, 1969.

Gilman, Richard. *The Making of Modern Drama: A Study of Büchner, Ibsen, Strindberg, Chekhov, Pirandello, Brecht, Beckett, Handke,* pp. 157–89. New York: Farrar, Straus & Giroux, 1974.

Krutch, Joseph Wood. "Pirandello and the Dissolution of the Ego." In *"Modernism" in Modern Drama: A Definition and an Estimate.* Ithaca, N.Y.: Cornell University Press, 1953.

MacClintock, Lander. *The Age of Pirandello.* Bloomington: Indiana University Press, 1951.

Paolucci, Anne. *Pirandello's Theater: The Recovery of the Modern Stage for Dramatic Art.* Carbondale: Southern Illinois University Press, 1974.

Ragusa, Olga. *Luigi Pirandello.* New York: Columbia University Press, 1968.

Starkie, Walter. *Luigi Pirandello.* London: J. M. Dent, 1926; 3d. rev. ed., Berkeley: University of California Press, 1965.

Tulane Drama Review (Spring 1966), 10(3):30–112. Special issue on Pirandello.

Vittorini, Domenico. *The Drama of Luigi Pirandello.* London: Oxford University Press; Philadelphia: University of Pennsylvania Press, 1935; reprint: New York: Dover Publications, 1957.

Genet

Abel, Lionel. "Metatheater: *Le Balcon.*" *Partisan Review* (1960), 27(2):324–30.
Brustein, Robert. *The Theatre of Revolt: Studies in Modern Drama from Ibsen to Genet,* pp. 361–412. Boston: Little, Brown, 1962.
Chiaramonte, Nicola. "Jean Genet: White and Black." *Partisan Review* (1961), 28(5–6):662–68.
Clark, Eleanor. "The World of Jean Genet." *Partisan Review* (1949), 16(4):442–48.
Coe, Richard N. *The Vision of Jean Genet: A Study of His Poems, Plays and Novels.* New York: Grove Press, 1968.
Coe, Richard N., ed. *The Theater of Jean Genet: A Casebook.* New York: Grove Press, 1970.
Driver, Tom F. *Jean Genet.* New York: Columbia University Press, 1966.
Ehrmann, Jacques. "Genet's Dramatic Metamorphosis: From Appearance to Freedom." *Yale French Studies* (Spring-Summer 1962), 29:33–42.
Eskin, Stanley. "Theatricality in the Avant-Garde Drama: A Reconsideration of a Theme in the Light of *The Balcony* and *The Connection.*" *Modern Drama* (1964), 7:213–22.
Esslin, Martin. *The Theatre of the Absurd,* pp. 166–97. Rev. ed. Garden City, N.Y.: Doubleday, 1969. Earlier edition, 1961.
Fowlie, Wallace. "The Art and Conscience of Jean Genet." *Sewanee Review* (1964), 72:342–48.
Grossvogel, David I. *The Blasphemers: The Theater of Brecht, Ionesco, Beckett, Genet,* pp. 133–74. Ithaca, N.Y.: Cornell University Press, 1965. First published as *Four Playwrights and a Postscript,* 1962.
Guicharnaud, Jacques, with June Guicharnaud. *Modern French Theatre: From Giraudoux to Genet,* pp. 259–78. Rev. ed. New Haven: Yale University Press, 1967. Earlier edition, *Modern French Theatre,* 1960.
Jacobsen, Josephine and William R. Mueller. *Ionesco and Genet: Playwrights of Silence.* New York: Hill & Wang, 1968.
Kelly, Morris, ed. *Genet/Ionesco: The Theatre of the Double.* New York: Bantam Books, 1959.
Knapp, Bettina L. *Jean Genet.* New York: Twayne, 1968.
Markus, Thomas B. "Genet, the Theatre of the Perverse." *Educational Theatre Journal* (1962), 14:209–14.
—— "The Psychological Universe of Jean Genet." *Drama Survey* (1964), 3:386–92.
McAuley, Gay. "The Problem of Identity: Theme, Form and Theatrical

Method in *Les Nègres, Kaspar* and *Old Times*." *Southern Review* (Adelaide) (March 1975), 8:51–65.

McMahon, Joseph H. *The Imagination of Jean Genet*. New Haven: Yale University Press, 1963.

Melcher, Edith. "The Pirandellism of Genet." *French Review* (October 1962), 36:32–36.

Oxenhandler, Neal. "Can Genet Be Saved? Remarks on *The Blacks*." *Contemporary Literature* (Autumn 1975), 16:417–32.

Pronko, Leonard Cabell. *Avant-Garde: The Experimental Theatre in France*, pp. 140–53. Berkeley: University of California Press, 1966.

Reck, Rima D. "Appearance and Reality in Genet's *Le Balcon*." *Yale French Studies* (Spring-Summer 1962), 29:20–25.

Sartre, Jean-Paul. Preface to *The Maids*. In Jean Genet, *The Maids and Deathwatch*, pp. 7–31. Rev. ed., Bernard Frechtman, trans. New York: Grove Press, 1961.

—— *Saint Genet: Actor and Martyr*. Bernard Frechtman, trans. New York: George Braziller, 1963. First published by Gallimard, Paris, as *Saint Genet: Comédien et Martyr*, 1952.

Swander, Homer D. "Shakespeare and the Harlem Clowns: Illusion and Comic Form in Genet's *The Blacks*." *The Yale Review* (December 1965), 55(2):209–27.

Thody, Philip. *Jean Genet: A Study of His Novels and Plays*. New York: Stein & Day; London: Hamish Hamilton, 1968.

Tonelli, Franco. "From Illusion to Theatre: Artaud and Genet." *Theatre Annual* (1973), 29:7–18.

Tulane Drama Review (Spring 1963), vol. 7, no. 3. Special issue on Genet and Ionesco.

Wellwarth, George E. *The Theater of Protest and Paradox: Developments in the Avant-Garde Drama*, pp. 113–33. New York: New York University Press, 1964.

Zimbardo, R. A. "Genet's Black Mask." *Modern Drama* (1965), 8:247–58.

Beckett

Barnard, G. C. *Samuel Beckett: A New Approach: A Study of the Novels and Plays*. New York: Dodd, Mead, 1970.

Brater, Enoch. "Brecht's Alienated Actor in Beckett's Theater." *Comparative Drama* (Fall 1975), 9:195–205.

—— "The 'Absurd' Actor in the Theatre of Samuel Beckett." *Educational Theatre Journal* (May 1975), 27(2):197–207.

Busi, Frederick. "Creative Self-Deception in the Drama of Samuel Beckett." *Research Studies* (Washington State University) (September 1974), 42:153–60.

Chevigny, Bell Gale, ed. *Endgame: A Collection of Critical Essays*. Englewood Cliffs, N.J.: Prentice-Hall, 1969.

Cohn, Ruby. *Samuel Beckett: The Comic Gamut*. New Brunswick, N.J.: Rutgers University Press, 1962.

Cohn, Ruby, ed. *Casebook on Waiting for Godot.* New York: Grove Press, 1967.
—— *Samuel Beckett: A Collection of Criticism.* New York: McGraw-Hill, 1975.
Copeland, Hannah C. *Art and the Artist in the Works of Samuel Beckett.* The Hague: Mouton, 1975.
Esslin, Martin. *The Theatre of the Absurd,* pp. 11–65. Rev. ed. Garden City, N.Y.: Doubleday, 1969. Earlier edition, 1961.
Esslin, Martin, ed. *Samuel Beckett: A Collection of Critical Essays.* Englewood Cliffs, N.J.: Prentice-Hall, 1965.
Fletcher, John and John Spurling. *Beckett: A Study of His Plays.* New York: Hill & Wang, 1972.
Friedman, Melvin J., ed. *Samuel Beckett Now: Critical Approaches to His Novels, Poetry, and Plays.* Chicago: University of Chicago Press, 1970.
Gilman, Richard. *The Making of Modern Drama: A Study of Büchner, Ibsen, Strindberg, Chekhov, Pirandello, Brecht, Beckett, Handke,* pp. 234–66. New York: Farrar, Straus & Giroux, 1974.
Grossvogel, David I. *The Blasphemers: The Theater of Brecht, Ionesco, Beckett, Genet,* pp. 85–132. Ithaca, N.Y.: Cornell University Press, 1965. First published as *Four Playwrights and a Postscript,* 1962.
Guicharnaud, Jacques, with June Guicharnaud. *Modern French Theatre: From Giraudoux to Genet,* pp. 230–58. Rev. ed. New Haven: Yale University Press, 1967.
Hayman, Ronald. *Samuel Beckett.* New York: Frederick Ungar, 1973.
Hoffman, Frederick J. *Samuel Beckett: The Language of Self.* Carbondale: Southern Illinois University Press, 1962.
Jacobsen, Josephine and William R. Mueller. *The Testament of Samuel Beckett.* New York: Hill & Wang, 1964.
Jones, Louisa. "Narrative Salvation in *Waiting for Godot.*" *Modern Drama* (June 1974), 17:179–88.
Journal of Modern Literature (February 1977), vol. 6, no. 1. Special issue on Beckett.
Kern, Edith. "Drama Stripped for Inaction: Beckett's *Godot.*" *Yale French Studies* (Winter 1954–55), 14:41–47.
Mayoux, Jean J. *Samuel Beckett.* Harlow: Longman Group, for the British Council, 1976.
Piling, John. *Samuel Beckett.* London: Routledge & Kegan Paul, 1976.
Pronko, Leonard Cabell. *Avant-Garde: The Experimental Theatre in France,* pp. 22–58. Berkeley: University of California Press, 1966.
Scott, Nathan A. *Samuel Beckett.* New York: Hillary House, 1965.
Tindall, William York. *Samuel Beckett.* New York: Columbia University Press, 1964.
Webb, Eugene. *The Plays of Samuel Beckett.* Seattle: University of Washington Press, 1972.
Wellwarth, George E. *The Theater of Protest and Paradox: Developments in the Avant-Garde Drama,* pp. 113–33. New York: New York University Press, 1964.

Worth, Katharine, ed. *Beckett the Shape Changer: A Symposium.* London and Boston: Routledge & Kegan Paul, 1975.

Weiss

Best, Otto F. *Peter Weiss.* Ursule Molinaro, trans. New York: Frederick Ungar, 1976.
Esslin, Martin. *Reflections: Essays on Modern Theatre,* pp. 149–56. Garden City, N.Y.: Doubleday, 1971.
Enderstein, Carl. "The Symbiosis of the Arts and Peter Weiss's *Marat/Sade.*" Paper presented at Midwest Modern Language Association Convention, Milwaukee, 1970.
Haberl, F. P. "Peter Weiss's Documentary Theatre." *Books Abroad* (Summer 1969), 43(3):359–62.
Hilton, Ian. *Peter Weiss: A Search for Affinities.* London: Oswald Wolff, 1970.
Moeller, Hans-Bernhard. "German Theater 1964: Weiss' Reasoning in the Madhouse." *Symposium* (Summer 1966), 20:163–73.
Parham, Sidney F. "*Marat/Sade:* The Politics of Experience, or the Experience of Politics?" *Modern Drama* (September 1977), 20(3):235–50.
"Peter Weiss in Conversation with A. Alvarez." *Encore* (July/August 1965), 12(4):4–15.
Roloff, Michael. "An Interview with Peter Weiss." *Partisan Review* (Spring 1965), 32(2):220–33.
Schechner, Richard, ed. "*Marat/Sade* Forum (Peter Brook, Leslie Fiedler, Geraldine Lust, Norman Podhoretz, Ian Richardson, Gordon Rogoff), *Tulane Drama Review* (Summer 1966), 10(4):214–37.
Sontag, Susan. "Marat/Sade/Artaud." In *Against Interpretation and Other Essays,* pp. 163–74. New York: Farrar, Straus & Giroux, 1966. First published in *Partisan Review* (1965), 32(2):210–19.
Taëni, Rainer. "Chaos versus Order: The Grotesque in *Kaspar* and *Marat/Sade.*" *Dimension* (1969), 2(3):592–603.
White, J. "History and Cruelty in Peter Weiss's *Marat/Sade.*" *Modern Language Review* (1968), 63:437–48.

Albee

Amacher, Richard E. *Edward Albee.* New York: Twayne, 1969.
Baxandall, Lee. "The Theatre of Edward Albee." *Tulane Drama Review* (Summer 1965), 9:19–40.
Bigsby, C. W. E. *Confrontation and Commitment: A Study of Contemporary American Drama, 1959–1966.* Columbia: University of Missouri Press, 1968.
Bigsby, C. W. E., ed. *Edward Albee: A Collection of Critical Essays.* Englewood Cliffs, N.J.: Prentice-Hall, 1974.

Cohn, Ruby. *Edward Albee*. Minneapolis: University of Minnesota Press, 1969.
Debusscher, Gilbert. *Edward Albee: Tradition and Renewal*. Brussels: American Studies Center, 1967.
Driver, Tom. "What's the Matter With Edward Albee?" *The Reporter*, January 2, 1964; rpt. in Alvin B. Kernan, ed., *The Modern American Theater*, pp. 99–103. Englewood Cliffs, N.J.: Prentice-Hall, 1967.
Educational Theatre Journal (March 1973), 25(1):46–85. Special issue on Albee.
Flynn, Betty. "A Visit with Edward Albee" (interview). *Chicago Daily News* (Panorama), March 18, 1967, pp. 1–3.
Halpern, Max. "What Happens in Who's Afraid . . . ?" In William E. Taylor, ed., *Modern American Drama: Essays in Criticism*, pp. 129–43. Deland, Fla.: Everett/Edwards, 1968.
Hayman, Ronald. *Edward Albee*. New York: Frederick Ungar, 1973.
Hazard, Forrest E. "The Major Theme in Who's Afraid of Virginia Woolf?" *The CEA Critic* (December 1968), pp. 10–11.
Kemper, Robert Graham. "Allegory of the American Dream: Another View of Virginia Woolf," *The Christian Century*, October 5, 1966, pp. 1214–15.
Martin, Richard. "One v. One, or Two Against All? A Note on Edward Albee's Who's Afraid of Virginia Woolf?" *Die Neueren Sprachen* (October 1973), 72:535–38.
McDonald, Daniel. "Truth and Illusion in Who's Afraid of Virginia Woolf?" *Renascence* (Winter 1964), 17:63–69.
Meyer, Ruth. "Language: Truth and Illusion in Who's Afraid of Virginia Woolf?" *Educational Theatre Journal* (1968), 20:60–69.
Quinn, James P. "Myth and Romance in Albee's Who's Afraid of Virginia Woolf?" *Arizona Quarterly* (Autumn 1974), 30:197–204.
Rutenberg, Michael E. *Edward Albee: Playwright in Protest*. New York: DBS Publications, 1969; reprint: New York: Avon Books, 1970.

Stoppard

"Ambushes for the Audience: Towards a High Comedy of Ideas" (interview). *Theatre Quarterly* (May–July 1974), 4:3–17.
Babula, William. "The Play-Life Metaphor in Shakespeare and Stoppard." *Modern Drama* (1972), 15:279–81.
Berlin, Normand. "*Rosencrantz and Guildenstern Are Dead*: Theater of Criticism." *Modern Drama* (1973), 16:269–77.
Bigsby, C. W. E. *Tom Stoppard*. Harlow: Longman Group, for the British Council, 1976.
Brustein, Robert. "Waiting for Hamlet." In *The Third Theatre*, pp. 149–53. New York: Simon & Schuster, 1969.
Farish, Gillan. "Into the Looking-Glass Bowl: An Instant of Grateful Terror." *University of Windsor Review* (Spring-Summer 1975), 10:14–29.

Gianakaris, C. J. "Absurdism Altered: Rosencrantz and Guildenstern Are Dead." Drama Survey (Winter 1968–69), 7(1–2):52–58.
Hayman, Ronald. Tom Stoppard. London: Heinemann Educational Books; Totowa, N.J.: Rowman & Littlefield, 1977.
James, Clive. "Count Zero Splits the Infinitive: Tom Stoppard's Plays." Encounter (November 1975), 45(5):68–76.
Kennedy, Andrew K. "Old and New in London Now." Modern Drama (1969), 11:437–46.
Keyssar-Franke, Helene. "The Strategy of Rosencrantz and Guildenstern Are Dead." Educational Theatre Journal (March 1975), 27(1):85–97.
Levenson, Jill. "Views from a Revolving Door: Tom Stoppard's Canon to Date." Queens Quarterly (1971), 78:431–42.
Salter, Charles H. "Rosencrantz and Guildenstern Are Dead." In Hermann J. Weiand, ed., Insight IV: Analyses of Modern British and American Drama, pp. 144–50. Frankfurt: Hirschgraben, 1975.
Tynan, Kenneth. "Profiles (Tom Stoppard): Withdrawing with Style from the Chaos." The New Yorker, December 19, 1977, pp. 41ff.

Handke

Gilman, Richard. The Making of Modern Drama: A Study of Büchner, Ibsen, Strindberg, Chekhov, Pirandello, Brecht, Beckett, Handke, pp. 267–88. New York: Farrar, Straus & Giroux, 1974. First published in American Review (May 1973), 17:206–28.
Heissenbüttel, Helmut. "Peter Handke and His Writings." Universitas (English ed.) (1970), 12(3):243–51.
Hern, Nicholas. Peter Handke. London: Oswald Wolff, 1971; New York: Frederick Ungar, 1972.
Honsza, Norbert. "Peter Handke as a Dramatist." Universitas (English ed.) (1973), 15(3):261–66.
Joseph, Artur. "Nauseated by Language" (interview). The Drama Review (Fall 1970), 15(1):56–61. (Complete interview [in German] appears in Artur Joseph, Theater unter vier Augen: Gespräche mit Prominenten, pp. 27–39. Berlin: Kiepenheuer & Witsch, 1969.
Kesting, Marianne. "The Social World as Platitude." Dimension (1969), 2:177–81.
Lederer, William L. "Handke's Ride." Chicago Review (1974), 26(2):171–76.
Lottman, H. R. "Two Authors, Two Points of View: Peter Handke, Hans Hellmut Kirst" (interview). Publishers Weekly (September 12, 1977), 212(11):54–56.
Mandel, Siegfried. Group 47: The Reflected Intellect. Carbondale: Southern Illinois University Press, 1973.
Peymann, Claus. "Directing Handke." The Drama Review (June 1972), 16(2):48–54.
Roloff, Michael. "Postscript: A Note on Methods." In Peter Handke, The

Innerworld of the Outerworld of the Innerworld, pp. 155–68. New York: Seabury Press, 1974.

Schlueter, June. "Peter Handke's *The Ride Across Lake Constance:* The Illusion of Self-Sufficiency." *Comparative Drama* (Summer 1977), 11(2):113–26.

Swift, Astrid. "The West German Theater Scene: 1966–1973." *Drama and Theatre* (Fall 1974), 12:2–11.

Weber, Carl. "Handke's Stage is a Laboratory." *The Drama Review* (June 1972), 16(2):55–62.

ꙅIndex